Three

An anthology of flash nonfiction

PushPen Press | Santa Cruz | San José | California

Three
An anthology of flash nonfiction

Edited by Steve "Spike" Wong, Jan McCutcheon, and Kelly A. Harrison

Featuring original work by Adnan Adnan, Ana Filomena Andrun, Kristen Austin, Linda Lee Ortiz Hughes Bakke, Terry Barr, Carlos Barron, Melissa Becker, Jesi Bender, Bri Bruce, Tess Crescini, Sage Curtis, Steve Cushman, Maria D'Avolio, Christopher Danaher, Kate Evans, Ashley Florimonte, Susan Forrest, Brian Foss, Nan Friedley, Erica Goss, Sebastien Grace, Kelly A. Harrison, Mark Heinlein, Belinda Hopkinson, Tram Huynh, Victoria M. Johnson, Morgan Kelly, Kylie Kenner, Thomas Leikam, Zac Locke, Gayle Lubeck, Amy Mackelden, Kathleen Maliksi, Jesse Mardian, Alex Marroquin, Mary Martine, Jane Matchak, Heather Matley, Greg Mayo, Jan McCutcheon, Jeri McCutcheon, Rose Marie McNair, Tonya McQuade, Shauna Miller, Roger Mock, Ume Naqvi, Sarju Naran, Nahida S. Nisa, Shirindokht Nourmanesh, Alexander Papoulias, Pranita Patel, Brandy Pech, Tara Phillips, Meg Pokrass, Yasmin Ramirez, Brownlee Reed, Kate Reid, Sarah Lyn Rogers, Jessica Sauceda, Evelyn A. So, Janie Vasquez, Daniel Wallock, Steve "Spike" Wong, Bryan Wong, Bob Woodward, Candice Wynne, Tim Yee

Library of Congress Cataloging-in-Publication Data is Available.
ISBN 978-0-9896676-2-3

All rights reserved. First edition November 8, 2014.
Revised December 17, 2014.

Printed in the United States of America.

EXECUTIVE EDITOR, ARTISTIC DIRECTOR, AND DECIDER IN CHIEF
Steve "Spike" Wong

MANAGING EDITOR
Jan McCutcheon

PRODUCTION EDITOR
Kelly A. "Eagle Eye" Harrison

EDITORS
Sage Curtis
Erica Goss
Alex Marroquin
Tara Phillips
Sarah Lyn Rogers

PROOFREADER
Susan McLucas

COVER DESIGN & PAGE LAYOUT
Jan McCutcheon

Dedicated to the memory of my mom, Alice Chin Wong, who was delighted by the fact that I thought the hippos were real on Disneyland's Jungle Cruise. She inspired me to always believe.

—Spike

Contents

Steve "Spike" Wong

Introduction

I'm going to say it right now: PushPen Press isn't interested in publishing boxing matches; we want Bruce Lee's one-inch punch.

Flash nonfiction is a genre that focuses the pith and power of nonfiction into those one-inch punches. We carry that idea a few steps further by creating constraints and challenges to focus the writing even more, to add a little juice to the creative efforts of our contributors.

For *Three*, we created…three flash nonfiction writing challenges: a story in three paragraphs, not to exceed three typewritten pages; a story in three haiku (itself a poetry poem in three lines), or a story in three black-and-white photos. Granted, we stretched the definition of "flash" a bit, but we are fine with that because our writers utilized the form to their advantage.

We allowed our writers to push the envelope of paragraph construction. Conservative English teachers will not be happy. Look at the paragraphs not in a mechanical sense, but see them as chapters in the story.

Haiku aficionados take note: we did not hold our writers to an exact, precise syllable count, nor did we demand adherence to traditional haiku requirements or techniques. One of the unique requirements we put on our haiku writers, trying to get them to see their words in a different light, was to submit a black-and-white photograph (that they had taken) to illustrate something about their work. All photos are copyrighted by the respective authors.

PushPen Press is passionate about empowering people to believe in their visions, life lessons, and storytelling. May *Three* inspire you to join us in this journey through life.

1

Sarah Lyn Rogers

Butterfly weather

O n a January morning, mellow-mild, you fly to the butterfly grove. The air fogs the windshield of your car, where you sit with your friends, riding the highway south. This is a fine time, you think; masses of butterflies are said to overwinter from October to February. You hope to collect the experience like a postcard: *Here we are, that time we saw the Monarchs thick like orange-brown leaves on the pines.* You want to record the snapshot in writing. In the car, you aim to kill two birds with one stone, put the cart before the horse, and other idioms, composing the haiku in your head on the drive: *Today the Monarchs/ reigned. On their migration path, / we clustered with them.*

There are no butterflies. When you arrive in Pacific Grove, it is fifty-five degrees and misty. *This temperature suspends their animation,* you read on a placard in the wingless sanctuary space. Whoever's there is hidden, but you look anyway. Hard. Everyone in your party thinks they see one, everyone but you, catching them flickering in the treetops or zipping into shadow between leaves. *No orange wings. Mist/ suspends animation; cold/ Monarchs do not reign.* You linger, hope to change the outcome with your will. Isn't this the way with plans? You have no control, the day continues. Slink back to the car.

The day is not over. Drive to the churning tide, to that crash of water smashed against the rocks. Picnic in the grey, grey air, your skin and hair dampening as the hazy sunlight fades to nothing. Breathe. Gather small stones. Revel in this blessing, this planlessness, the wide expanse of sky and sea, the lines of birds, the puddles and precarious boulders to climb, carefully. Scrap your preconceptions. Scrap the rigid form. You haven't earned the wisdom of brevity; you need more words for what little you have to say. Grey twilight and shoes full of sand. It wasn't the plan, but look, look what you were given.

Shauna Miller

Home base

Shauna Miller

Melissa Becker

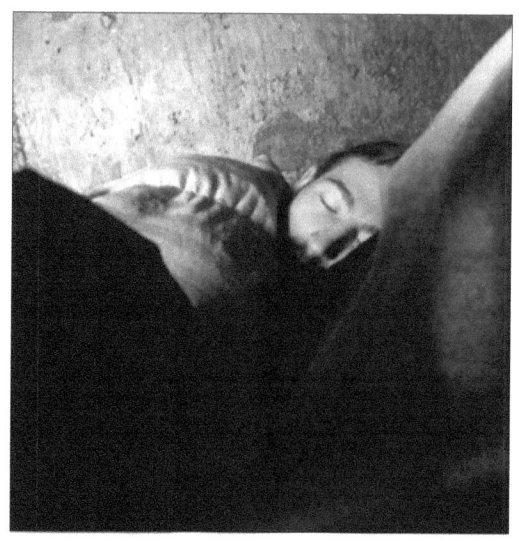

Shared love paracosm

Scratches on wood-
An eager cat looks out the window
At a waking bird.

A small quiet snore-
Bonded by soul, he sleeps by me
In the gray morn light.

Warmth draped over us-
The blanket offers comfort
As I dream awake.

Adnan Adnan

Thirty-two eyes

These thieves are unlucky. They are caught very early in the morning, in a cattle-bazaar. In Bangladesh it is almost customary to beat a thief before you call the police, when you catch one. If the thief is lucky, he gets caught in a neighborhood, and he is taken to an open field, where he is beaten by a few able men for an hour or two. But if he is unlucky, he gets caught in a bazaar, and he is beaten by everyone, for hours. And if he is really unlucky, he gets caught in a cattle-bazaar, very early in the morning, and he is beaten until the evening, sometimes well into the night, even by the people who, after hearing the news of the capture, come from neighboring towns or villages just to beat them. If this is your thing and you are adventurous, then you could witness at least one of these events if you travel across Bangladesh before any national or religious celebration. Most Bengalis grow up seeing this at least once a year. To us it's nothing new, nothing unusual – it's normal. We are good people. If you are our guest, you will never forget the quality of our hospitality. But you must never get caught stealing, because that is when some of us turn into cheerful torturers and murderers.

It is now only two days to go before the *Eid-Al-Adha* (Festival of Sacrifice), and every single cow must be sold. Maybe there are still too many cows to be sold, and the owners and businessmen are worried, and not able to sleep at night, in the open bazaar under the open sky, where the air smells like cow dung and urine. It's barely dawn when they find out that on the other side of the bazaar 16 thieves are caught. When the cow owners get there, they find a big circle of people, and in the middle of it they see 16 men tied together in a small and tight circle with a long rope. They are tied in a way that they face the people, their hands touching each others' hands behind them. They are all alive, but their eyes are dead, still looking for mercy, knowing that it will not come. Don't worry. This is still normal. It is hot, and everyone is thinking how they should go about it and be done with it. Should they beat the men one by one or in groups? They are used to beating one or two thieves at a time, maybe three or four, but almost never this many. They feel that they must plan for it in such a way that will guarantee an exemplary beating; it must be something that people will talk about for years to come. No one talks to the thieves. No one bothers to even look at them, at their eyes. All 16 of them are begging for mercy, but everyone else hears it as noise, just noise. "Why don't we pull their eyes out?" The young man's question doesn't even bring about a tiny silence, which you may have expected. Instead, the crowd shouts in agreement. This is still normal. No one really knows how it is going to end. The owner of the cows realizes things are moving in an unpleasant direction. "These are my cows," he says. "Please let me decide what to do. My cows are not stolen. I lost nothing. I will just call the police, and let them decide." But the young man disagrees. "We need to set an example," he says. There are others like them. Maybe even in this crowd. We need to pull their eyes out to send a message." He sends a boy to bring a spoon from a nearby tea-stall. He looks at the spoon and says, "Small, but it will do." For many it is the end of the fun. They start to leave, not even realizing that even they had their hands into what is to come next. But some stay to see the end, to see the pulled-out eyes.

When the young man pulls out the first eye, there is a scream, which is heard even from the very back of the cattle-bazaar. A few of the thieves shit and piss in their *lungis*. But the young man keeps pulling the eyes out very quickly, like an athlete, like in a competition. Some of the thieves beg, "Just pull one of my eyes, and let me have the other one… *baba* forgive me." But before these thieves are done making their cases, the young man is done. He is already holding the eyes in a small bucket that the businessmen usually use to piss in at night. When the police arrive, no one can tell anything about the young man who pulled the eyes out, so they just hand over he 16 thieves and their 32 eyes in a bucket, eyes still trying to look up from the crowded bloody bottom, witnessing nothing.

Maria D'Avolio

Treasures

D irt poor is how my grandmother started her life. She grew up in a hovel in a village in Sicily, and WWII brought with it further deprivation. Almost a decade after her marriage she came to the US and by the time I came on the scene, she'd escaped her humble beginnings and lived in an upper-class neighborhood in upstate New York. I remember the doorway that led to her attic and a world of mystery and excitement, my mother's wedding dress being one of the first treasures we'd find crammed into the small space. The cellar, was sinister: dank, musty, and jam-packed with junk Grandma saved everything; paint cans with only a tablespoon of paint left at the bottom; old bra strap hooks; underwear elastic that she could re-use, like the BVD elastic she put into the pleated skirt she made for one of my Aunties. She mended and repaired her sheets until they looked like a patchwork quilt, saving the replacement sheets my mother and her siblings had given her, until she really needed them. When Grandma had to be moved to a nursing home for dementia, they found the sheets in the cupboards, still wrapped in their original packaging. They had to rent an industrial sized dumpster to dispose of the dried-out paint cans, furniture, used clothing and other things she had saved, relics that spoke of the past from which she had come.

Her oldest daughter, my mother, came from the same beginnings, and while she left Sicily after the war and came to the US at age eight, she did not have a lot as a child. "Maria," she's admonished me as she's pulled one-inch carrot ends and celery leaves from my garbage, "it's obvious you did not grow up with scarcity! Those would have been the base for a soup for my entire family!" I feel bad for the waste, but cast aside the vestiges of Italian Catholic guilt along with all the other useless items from my marriage and former life. My mother's house is not that of a hoarder, but it is the opposite of Spartan, with every surface covered in knickknacks, books, plants and hundreds of pictures of her kids and grandkids.

And then there's my teenage daughter who makes me wonder if there is a genetic component to "conserving." She obviously did not live through the deprivation that both her grand and great-grandmothers did, yet she cannot bear to part with anything, be it the rock collection from her preschool years, or her favorite dress from kindergarten. "Mom! That's my favorite," she'll tell me indignantly, as she stops me from pitching a broken shell or a ticket stub, in my attempts to help her organize." Her bedroom shares many of the traits I remember from my grandmother's house, sans the paint cans, but with the addition of clothes, half-eaten food, old school projects, and a jumble of other items that I'd rather avoid looking at, scattered across her room. But in this, I also see the transition from my grandmother conserving from necessity, to my mother's sentimentality, and then my daughter who cannot bear to part with the simple things from her childhood that have meant something to her, maybe a clinging to the past when life felt simpler. Well... if you don't include the mess on the floor! The rest of my house is austere in comparison to the three of them, and I wonder how this tendency to collect skipped me. Just don't look in my garage or my three sheds!

Broadmoor boy

B etween the ages of seven and ten I lived in a hotel. Not any hotel but the five-star rated Broadmoor resort hotel in Colorado in a chapter of my life I seldom if ever say much about because people hearing it tend to say, "Oh, so you were a really spoiled rich kid." No, it's just that my parents couldn't find suitable housing. The company my father worked for also owned the hotel and so we moved into a double suite.

I got to know every inch of the place from the massive boiler room to the catacombs where all the ghostly relics of old furniture and fixtures rested covered in thick spider webs. In summer, it was a two-minute walk from our suite to the swimming pool. In winter, a five-minute walk to the ice rink. Any time of year the hotel's soda fountain was seconds away and a certain refuge. Along the way I met Benny Okatawa. His parents worked at the hotel and we became fast friends. Our bond was exploration. Years later I found out that Benny had spent much of his early childhood in an internment camp. I was sad to learn that he had to endure that.

In summer, the Texans and Oklahomans arrived to fill the hotel's rooms. They talked louder and faster than most people I'd ever known and tended to call me "sonny." Come winter, fewer people were around the hotel. One of the winter guests stood out because he had an odd squeaky voice. And when he said my name it didn't come out Bobby but "Baubee." I hadn't thought much about that man until my dad took me to the local arts theater some years later to see "It's A Wonderful Life." As the film rolled, I heard that voice again. "Oh," my father murmured in the darkened theater, "that's Mr. Stewart. He stayed down the hall from us once."

White fury

O ne of my fondest memories is horseback riding in Cloverdale, California. All of the kids had selected their horses while avoiding the ones that frightened them for some reason. I was the last to choose, and ended up with the most spirited horse of all. It was a white mare with blue eyes, and long, lush blond eyelashes. The fire in those orbs, and the snort of her snout, as she nodded to me while she brushed her right hoof into the dirt, indicated trouble. This was my steed.

The journey started out benignly enough. We went on a serene mountain trail through the woodlands. I remember the sounds of the hooves hitting the dirt, the earthy smells, and the light gently protruding through the otherwise dark forest. I can still hear the directives of my teacher, as she let us know where to turn and kept us together. My mare turned to look at me occasionally to let me know she was the boss. I felt the intensity from her quick glances. Those blue eyes contained remnants of the sparkle of all equine that have gone before her, equally primordial and familiar. Past meeting present in the glimmers.

After about 40 minutes, I noticed she was giving me a rougher ride than before. We hastened upon a meadow after the woods ended. With a gallop and a stir she began to break away from the pack. I felt this animal swiftly gain momentum. I began to scream. I had never felt the energy of a horse so substantially as in that moment. She had her own agenda. I heard the gasps of the others. I was petrified then, but looking back now; I feel that I would like to take a rapid ride on a thoroughbred again. Although this time, it would be intentional.

Jan McCutcheon

The waiting and how we endured it

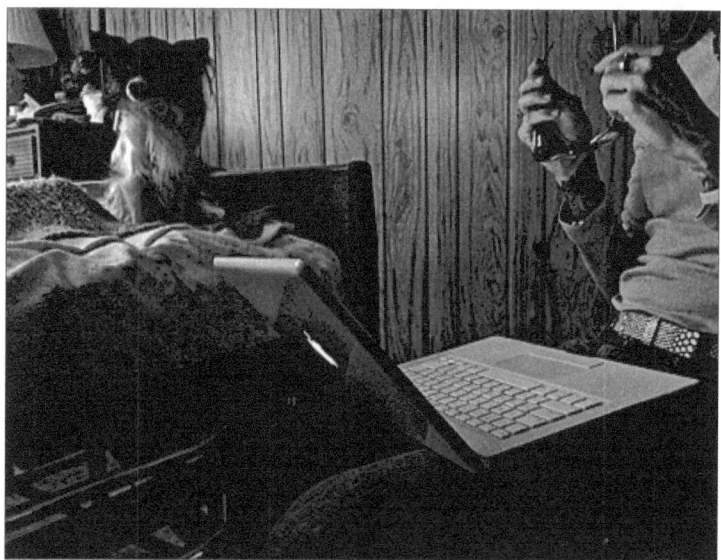

The waiting and how we endured it

The girls' room

G rowing up I shared the bedroom in the house on Washington Street with my sister who was six years older than me. The large bedroom had big windows that I liked to gaze out from (even though the view was just our neighbor's house), an adjoining bathroom where I liked to take long baths, and a spacious closet where I sometimes escaped to for quiet time. If my brothers made me mad or the house got too loud I would step in and close the door and sit in the safety of the cool darkness. Of all the rooms in our quirky old 1920's house, I appreciated the closet most. Not that I had many clothes, and actually my sister's things filled 90% of the space. Rather, the closet had a secret passage that led to the huge closet in my Mom's master bedroom. Whenever company came over to play I'd slip past my sister's sleek dresses and her fragrant sweaters, step over her neat rows of leather boots, moccasins, and strappy sandals in every color. My playmates could never find me because I'd creep from my Mom's room to the backyard. I never told any of them the secret to our closet. The closet was also my safe place to hide if aliens or monsters ever came to our house. I believed in both.

My sister had Beatles posters everywhere in our bedroom—to the point where you couldn't see the walls. Every morning I'd wake up to George Harrison smiling at me. He was my favorite Beatle. The room was where her friends would sit and chat, gossip, and laugh. I was like an invisible ghost. No one ever seemed to notice me there, sitting and pretending to read or pretending to do homework, so I was privy to all the conversations. One liked a boy; the boy liked her, too. Another had a dad that wouldn't let her wear short skirts so she waited until she got to school to roll up her skirt, and a third wanted to copy the look of a celebrity from a teen magazine for the school dance. My sister wanted to learn to kiss. I didn't understand the fuss they made over boys and clothes. A friend named Ana asked about me on her first visit, and my sister seemed surprised that anyone would mind my presence. She said to Ana, "Oh, don't worry, she can keep a secret." So Ana sat on the edge of the bed and told everyone how she went to the movies with a boy even though her mom thought she was only taking her little sister. "I sat her next to other kids in the front row and we sat a few rows back," she said. "And we made out."

The girls also played music and did each other's hair and makeup. They ratted their hair, and they wore eyeliner all around the eyes, Cleopatra-like. I enjoyed watching them and longed for the time when I would wear makeup and style my hair. I had no style at all and my hair was usually a tangled mess.

Like Paul, John, George, and Ringo, I became a good observer, silent, unquestioning. I became good at blending in with the walls. Later, when my sister started dating—unbeknownst to our Mom—the room was where she would talk on the phone, and sometimes it was where she would cry in her pillow. Once because I was so very invisible, she even took a bunch of pills to end her life. She was sobbing because her boyfriend had broken up with her. "You better not tell anyone," she said to me. I nodded but I had heard the front door open and close, so I left the room. It was my brother, and for the first time, I spoke about what I'd seen in the room. I told a secret. My brother called the ambulance. And though some dumb boy was the one who broke her heart, I knew my sister would never forgive me.

Tonya McQuade

Contrasts

Landing in L.A.,
I am oddly overcome
By its open space.

Memories crowd in
Of Osaka—two years home—
Sky scrapers, train tracks,

Breathing cigarettes,
Ingesting noise, pounding rock...
Craving nature's peace.

Metastasizing

Thoughts sail on the smoke
Of summertime gluttony
Infatuation

Sunlight hurts my eyes
From my pupils being wide
Love, forgive my sins

I pray life restarts
But apologies are tired
And so is my heart

Shirindokht Nourmanesh

Walls never lie

The room was lost in the gloom and shadows of midnight. The house was taken by silence and I felt alone. Then came his stabbing snore from the couch, from the living room, from the other side of the house, from a far away distance, from an unfamiliar life—a so-called married life—passing through the walls, reaching, reaching to my bed—our bed, icy cold, heavy, brutal—savagely, uncompromisingly brutal. I waited, listening; stretched out on bed listening to the loud and heavy breathing that came to me from the other side of the house—drunk, scratched, strange, cruel, vicious —savagely, uncompromisingly vicious. How long has it been? How long has it been for this noise—for this unfamiliar noise—to reach me from the other side of the house, from the top of the couch?

I moved a bit and turned to my left, and suddenly my body mounted a miniature hill it had created on the mattress by its own weight and climbed into the coldness and hardness of the other side; and I froze in dread and wonder. I felt my heart sinking deep into the darkness crashing against the walls, breaking into pieces. Under my half-naked body, there was the chill of the mattress trembling around my neglected Being, and my heart aflame of all this foul play. I twisted around myself, like a wounded deer left to die at the side of the road, like a smashed bird under the weight of a car. I tossed and turned and my face burned with tears erupting out of my eyes, and now my cry was even louder than his snore, my chest beating into the air, drumming away the seconds. *"In my loneliness,"* I wrote a few days later, *"The need to want is as useless / As a cry in the wind, and the / Desire, like the rush of termites, eats / Me from within."*

I knew someone was there; walls never lie. Someone had been in my house, had walked around and had gone through my belongings, and this person's unfamiliar presence was still hanging from the walls—persistent, stubborn. I knew someone had come with the outmost impudence and audacity, and in the privacy of my house had wrapped his or her body around my partner's, and Bang! There I was smashed into a wall—hard. This person's alien presence felt like a heavy slap on my face—like spite, like hatred, like pain. This person had gone through the most private corner of my home and had left a red curly hair on my hairbrush and on the seat of the toilet as a token of his or her pleasure. This person's presence was still dripping from the shower stall, and I was left alone in the middle of the room while walls were stripping out to the distance, were vanishing into the darkness of my surroundings, and were separating from each other—changing their green into the color of blood. And I in the middle of the room felt like one wandered astray in an awfully dark, gloomy jungle. I sat down on the hardness of the mattress and moved my hand under the blanket in search of anything unfamiliar; then I bent over the bed, put my nose to the surface and smelled it expecting a stink. I sat there for a while and kept asking myself *why*, until my feet reached the closet and my hands started packing.

Jan McCutcheon

Fifty shades of bruised

We wonder if the next doctor visit will alert the National Domestic Violence Hotline. We are the walking wounded and we are strong.

We have symmetrical bruises on our hips and collar bones, whip marks on our calves, thighs, and arms, rug burns on our asses, scraps and bruises on our shins, and callouses on our hands. We belong to the cult of CrossFit. We are stronger than we've ever been and continue to get stronger every week. We don't give up. We wear our scars as badges of courage; these are the markings of our tribe. Our community respects a nice six-inch shin scrape. They nod and say, "Yeah, box-jumps are a bitch." We laugh with a person when they are cursing the wicked jump rope, which is really a metal cable that slashes when it hits skin. We never laugh *at* them because we all know that pain. We push through the pain because we are learning that our brains say *can't* much too soon. Our bodies are capable of more. We are testing our limits and it's personal. Every situp, pushup, and pullup counts. Each breakthrough is celebrated. When I accomplish my first rope climb, I am exhilarated. I am 12 feet above the ground, but it feels like 40 and I'm not sure how I'll get down. My hands are sweating and barely large enough to go around the thick rope. It leaves brush burns where it touches my legs. The surface is grimy with the skin and sweat of the others who climbed before me. I am still afraid of heights. Every. Single. Time. I climb anyway.

We end each workout, flat on our backs, leaving a sweat angel on the black rubber flooring. We lie there gasping for breath and say things like, "Damn. That was hard." Then we get up, smile at our comrades and say, "Good work. See you tomorrow, right?" I plan my next goal: ten strict pullups.

Pacific

He is the block bad boy at the 41st Avenue Hook. Brash. Impulsive. A rough neck. Surfers tame him sometimes, but he'll take a life or a city at will, a rapacious sea.

There is that uncommon day, that windless, waveless, sunlit day when all the bluster stops, and the sea turns introspective and timid. And in the stillness you can hear him screaming for his life, a pacifist without power of his own, his fierce ragings forced upon him by his tormentors: heat and wind and gravity; subterranean quakes; and the massive gyres of the globe; and us. These rankle and enrage. Not the pacific sea. Not the fragile, fearful sea.

Just off shore a disinterested, buoyantly red Doritos bag circles and circles in its half life.

Bryan Wong

Reluctant Witness

The bell sounded in early evening, right after we had eaten dinner. The dispatcher's terse voice sounded scratchy through the speaker. "Engine Two, report of a medical emergency, on South Cragmont Avenue, for a 43-year-old female patient with abdominal pain." The four of us assigned to the engine headed out of the day room and climbed aboard. Willie, the engineer, blasted the traffic with the air horn and siren to clear a path onto the ever busy Alum Rock Avenue and headed toward the foothills, with the reflection of the flashing red lights bouncing off passing cars and buildings as we sped east. Drivers of cars hurriedly jerked to the right to give us the right of way with our noisy, wailing approach; a look I've heard described compared to Moses' parting of the Red Sea. We pulled up in front of a 1950's era house that looked well worn and sorely in need of some new paint and landscaping. We grabbed our medical gear from the side compartment and hastily strode into the house, where we were greeted by several cheerful family members who were watching a game show playing loudly on TV. "She's back in the bedroom!" said a little boy about eight years old, pointing towards a hallway. The family seemed more focused on the TV show than the fact that emergency personnel were barging into their house. Charlotte (my fellow firefighter) and I entered a small bedroom that was cramped with a dresser drawer and a bed that was too large for the room. A Mexican-American woman, who appeared about 40-years old, was lying on top of the bed, dressed in street clothes. The patient seemed to be in a moderate amount of pain, grimacing and holding her lower abdomen and groaning "Ay, Ay" as the spasms of pain coursed through her. The patient's daughter, who appeared to be about 13-years old, stood in the corner of the room, sobbing uncontrollably. Charlotte took the patient's daughter aside to calm her down and ask questions that might give us more information regarding her mother's medical history, as I continued my exam of the patient. She had lower abdominal pain that had increased over the past several hours; no history of trauma or injury to that area, no swelling, but painful to the touch. No blood in her stools or urine. She had not eaten anything unusual in the past several hours. No vomiting. No cardiac history. Not pregnant. I took her vital signs, applied some oxygen, and placed her on the cardiac monitor to check her heart rate and rhythm. As the ambulance crew arrived, I gave them the information I had gathered and assisted the patient to the gurney in the hallway.

Charlotte grabbed my arm and motioned for me to step back away from the gurney so that the patient would not hear us talking. "Hey," she whispered. "I found out why the daughter is so upset. Just before we got here, she called her daughter into the room and told her that she was diagnosed with ovarian cancer about a year ago and it has metastasized. No one else in the family knows. She couldn't take the pain anymore and that's why she called 911. She just told her daughter 'I'm going to die pretty soon and now you have to be a grown-up and be in charge of your little brother.' That's the kid in the living room." My mind reeled at the enormity of that information. "Wow," I said, "she didn't even tell *me* that she had cancer; that was kind of important." Aside from being relevant from a clinical aspect, I could not begin to fathom the explosive, emotional bombshell that had just been dropped upon the teenage daughter minutes before our arrival. It still never ceases to amaze me that some of our patients will leave out pertinent details of their medical history for whatever reason; forgetfulness, embarrassment and/or ignorance of their condition. In this case, our patient chose privacy and secrecy. We quickly picked up our medical equipment and followed the medics down the hallway. As we passed through the living room, the relatives again greeted us with their cheerfulness. "Bye! We'll come pick you up at the hospital in a little while, okay?" they said to our patient. "Thanks, you guys!" to us as we headed out the door. A quick look and assumption told me I was probably looking at the patient's parents and brother, as well as her son. Charlotte and I glanced at each other, silently. I quietly spoke to the attending paramedic as he pushed the gurney into the ambulance. "My partner just told me that the patient has metastatic ovarian cancer. She didn't tell me; her daughter told us," I gestured toward the patient, who was looking a little more pale in the well-lit interior of the ambulance. "Well, that's just a small detail, isn't it?" he said with a wry smile that indicated he'd heard this story many times before. He shook his head as he climbed into the ambulance and slammed the door shut.

We quickly loaded our medical gear back into the side compartment and jumped back into the cab of the engine. "This is awful. Let's get out of here," remarked Charlotte as we got into the engine and drove away, back towards the station. "Yeah, really," I replied as I glanced back towards the house, realizing that we had just become reluctant witnesses to a sad and terrible secret that was soon to be told to the other family members in that living room. The whole thing felt worse to me because the patient's family was so cheerful and smiling during the entire event and that we knew something they didn't know, but would soon find out. Those effervescent smiles would soon be replaced by tears and sorrow, and for the daughter and her little brother, their lives were soon to change. I wondered who would have the heartbreaking duty of telling the family. I hoped that it would not fall upon the teenage daughter's shoulders. Perhaps I really didn't want to know.

Three

I can feel the warmth of the sun shining on my skin as I run up the steps to my grandparents' house. The house is old and I can see chips of paint peeling off from the sides of the house. I hurry inside, anxious to play with my cousins who are already there visiting. My grandfather, weak and dying of cancer, is lying on the couch watching TV as my grandmother feeds him. My cousins and I begin running through the house playing. I scoot past the bedroom to the left of the kitchen, where I see my uncle sitting on the edge of the bed watching TV. He motions me into the room. He never says a word, nor do I as he slides his hand where it shouldn't be. The look in my uncle's eyes tells me to stand still and remain quiet as he continues to move his hand in between my legs, fondling me. I knew in this moment that I was changed forever, and then he adjusts my pants, sending me out of the room. I want to run and cry, but instead I run off to play.

A few months later my grandfather passes away of cancer. My grandmother remarries and moves into the same neighborhood as mine. My new grandpa spoils me, buying me anything I wanted. He tells me often "You're so pretty; you're my favorite." He makes me feel so special, and oh, how I love him! When my grandparents return from a short trip to Reno, I can't wait to find out what they've brought me. My grandpa whispers "Come into the room with me; I have a special gift just for you. Don't tell the others, they might get jealous!" This is a gift to show me how much he loves me, he says. He has me remain quiet as he slides his hand down my panties. He takes my hand and places it down his pants, and he begins to breathe in my ear. Afterwards, I receive a big shiny silver dollar; he says it's because I was such a good girl. Over the years, I grow to hate the huge collection of silver dollars that my brother says I'm lucky to have. The despair I have is so overwhelming that I begin sneaking into my parents' liquor cabinet, drinking right from the bottle. I am just a dirty little girl, with dirty little secrets, and though I'm only nine, I make up my mind to end my life. In my parents' bathroom, I hold my dad's silver razor. I unscrew it from the bottom, hold the blade in my hand, and stare back and forth from the razor to my reflection in the mirror. An ugly good for nothing, no purpose piece of trash looks back at me. The tears stream down my face. I slash. Blood drips from my wrist, and somehow I know the cut isn't deep enough. I place the razor back, hating myself even more because I'm not strong enough to do away with this senseless life. Thus begins a journey of suicide attempts. Only once do I almost succeed. I'm 11, staring at that horrible face in the mirror, and this time I take pills by the handful. I feel myself drifting, my body becoming so heavy. How easy, easy I think, my escape. Darkness, then in the distance of my mind I hear a voice, "Janie, Janie, oh God what did you do?" I feel my body being shaken, then forced to vomit. Oh, why does she stop me, why does my cousin find me?

Right after eighth grade I begin dating the boy I will later marry. I still keep my secrets from him, but because of him, I don't hate myself as I once did. For the first time I am truly happy. We spend all summer together, talking on the phone when we can't see each other. One day as school begins, I walk by the swimming pool. I see five boys standing by the bathroom. "Don't go near them!" a voice inside me screams. I'm 13; I ignore it, these are my classmates, I know them. I hear "NOW" and I'm pulled into the bathroom! I'm thrown to the ground, held down, my legs and arms pinned, as one boy stands over me and begins to unbutton his pants. I had learned long ago to be quiet. With my head turned I whimpered, "Please don't, please don't." Why wasn't I worth anything? Am I only worth how others could demean me? My past now entwined with my present, or had it been all along? Why can't I find the strands to separate each aspect of my life? The drinking starts back up, as do the drugs, my only salvation from reality. My boyfriend hates who I am becoming. He gives me an ultimatum, drinking and drugs, or him. It's easy. I choose him, the one person who asks to hold my hand, to kiss me, asks for everything, and never takes. Later we would give birth to three children, and adopt three more. I was only three, a baby, when I was molested for the first time. Everything in threes, a number that holds all my secrets. I would share the secrets of that past with my husband, releasing only bits and pieces, for my nightmares came back after the birth of our first child. They are no longer secrets that I will take to the grave, but I am slow to tell nonetheless. I share one day with my aunt the things done to me by my grandfather. I tell her how he made me sit on the toilet once he was done. He would spread my legs and pour Pine-Sol on me, disinfecting me as if I were the dirty one. She cries as I tell her about the house on Lincoln Street and the bedroom to the left of the kitchen. Then she says, "Janie, you weren't three when grandma lived there. You were two."

Jeri McCutcheon

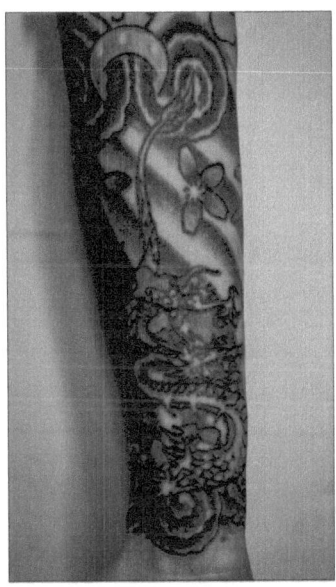

Arm dragon

purple rage anger
hatred burns wind and fire
ablaze, looming fear

blue dragon strong, true
unsuspecting deception
resistance collide

arise golden one
dragon lady triumphant
tranquil harmony

The gold country

After a year, his older cousins Jimmy and George sent word–California was a magnificent place. There were redwoods that touched the sky, oranges and apricots fell out of the trees into your hands, women like golden Amazons. There was work to be had by anyone who would ask for it. The young man went home for the last time and cried as he kissed his mother and father goodbye. He promised to send money.

He and his cousins picked cherries and apricots the first year. In the morning fog and the warm sun of California afternoons, they made their plans. The man went back to his little island five years later with a gold ring and an American wife. In California he was a mechanic, and he made more money than he'd ever dreamed of. The valley where they lived was perfect like a flower just before it blooms. He bought a little house with fruit trees in the yard, and had a car of his own. A Mustang with a radio in the dash. Soon there was a baby boy and the journey back home. He returned to his village like a conqueror and held his son up for everyone to see and to let him touch the grape vines that had hung outside the family house for a hundred years. In time there were two more boys and the visits home were always sweet and sad like life is. Always a goodbye waiting at the end.

When the man died his sons were not grown, but they crossed the sea to take their father home. They were heartsick, but the life he'd dreamt for them went on for the man's family. The boys took their mother back to that little island every few years and they were showered with kisses and wept over and fed like kings. The boys grew into men, and soon there was a new generation of cousins on that little island who dreamed of leaving, and they asked the men about their home. About California. They'd grown up with stories of the uncles who had left for the gold country, how they became tycoons in the valley of cherries and apricots. The men tried to explain but their words fell short–that valley was gone. The flower had bloomed and dropped its seeds and in its place, a concrete maze, a web of highways, an endless tract of identical shopping centers. A new kind of worker who had no use for the sun or the soil crowded in and filled every last open space. The valley their father found not so very long ago had vanished into the day like a dream you long to remember.

2

Hailstorm

A hailstorm interrupts the still morning, pit-patting on ground hardened with frost. Among other sights, the sky darkens, high clouds over black mountains, the sea a pale gray dimpled in wind. The brown hens settle in their boxes. The waxy leaves of the magnolia blanket the lawn.

The wet sheen of rain and sleet on your neck, you wander through rows of apple trees, nearly bare in winter. Only a few paces before looking back, perhaps you hesitate to continue without me. The unhappy winter chill does not remember the sun above, or the sweet bite of a ripe persimmon, even in autumn.

When the hail stops, you pause, tilting your head backward upon that same rain-wet neck and I see tomorrow, see poetry in the angle of your throat, then the ocean in your eyes, its tides pulsing in my veins.

Nahida S. Nisa

And I effuse

Take your breaking, slow,
All the universe is snow;
we rub like velvet,

sunlit glass; we peel
like an eyelash in the grass.
Violets brim wet.

When you and I wake,
the noon has come again to
let the sadness in.

Kathleen Maliksi

21 seconds

The view at 165 feet on a mountaintop is incomparable; green fields below and mountains and hills all around me. But it's hard to appreciate with rain beating down on the little wooden shelter, with a roof and no walls, which I'm huddled beneath. The harsh wind blows the rain in my direction anyway. I stare down at the two 350-meter-long pieces of rope that are my ticket down this mountain. I never thought I had a fear of heights; I'm starting to re-think that now. The people that I have climbed up the mountain with have abandoned me, deciding to make their way down through the same path we came up instead of taking the zip-line. I hesitate for half a second, wondering if I should take the longer but easier way out and follow them down. But my stubborn determination wins over. I paid to do the zip-line, so by God, I will do the zip-line, even if Mother Nature is against me. The rain starts to let up, until it stops completely and suddenly the sun is there again. It doesn't slowly emerge from its cloudy hiding place; it's just there, all glaring and mocking, daring me to run and hide now that I can't use the rain as an excuse to postpone my death-defying trip.

The days stretch on, one after the next. One week becomes two until it turns into a month. Everyone says it will get easier but it hasn't yet. How can it be easy when the person that I love is gone? When he's chosen to move on with his life without me? My days are haunted by the words he said, unspoken promises made. My nights are filled with memories of his touch and his kiss. Every part of my body still yearns for him…still belongs to him. I think about that mountaintop. Falling in love was like falling off that peak. I was jerked back and let go, the fall sudden and quick.

Twenty-one seconds. That is how long the trip down the zip-line takes. It is the fastest zip-line in the Philippines. The rope dips down like a slide and then evens out, carrying you across 350 meters in 21 seconds. Twenty-one seconds was how long it took for me to get from the top of that mountain to the ground. Twenty-one seconds was how long it took for me to get lost in his eyes on that first date. Still wet from the rain and the sun now shining in my eyes, I allow myself to be strapped into the harness. The requisite pictures are taken but I can't concentrate, all I can see is the grassland far below me and a cow in the middle of the field. If the zip-line malfunctions and I go falling to my death, I wonder if the cow will have enough sense to move away. Or maybe I'll go rolling into it, smack my head on the ground and scatter my guts all over that green grass. The cow will stand, unharmed, and wander on, grazing on the grass that's not stained red. All of this flashes through my mind in the few seconds that it takes the well-practiced and competent team to strap on my harness. I walk to the coffee place where we're supposed to meet. My hands are shaking, images flash in my mind of all the ways that it could and probably would go wrong. I arrive at our meeting spot and he's there, waiting for me. I'm being pulled back and let go. I hurtle down, my screams getting lost in the wind. Twenty-one seconds turns into 21 hours but all I can see is a blur of green, a flash of black as I pass over the cow. I make it to the other side, my body shaking from head to toe as I'm being unstrapped from the harness. Only 21 seconds have passed and I have traveled across 350 meters and 165 feet. Twenty-one seconds have passed and I'm looking across a table at a boy, his smile wide and contagious, his eyes lit up in a way that makes my heart pound faster. Twenty-one more seconds pass and I'm still falling through the air, no rope, no safety net at the bottom. There's a million ways that this could go wrong and I feel like, this time, I was thrown off the mountain against my will. The falling makes me feel free and alive; the crash to the ground will be the most painful thing I'll ever feel. The boy smiles at me and takes my hand. I close my eyes and enjoy the fall.

Meg Pokrass

The married man

When he called on the phone his voice was hard and tight. He said he was in trouble—that he was going back to X. He said she came by to go over the final divorce papers, and he couldn't.

The room felt too bright. Everything appeared unmovable. I looked at my ankles, covered with bug bites. They itched. I peered at my mother's kitchen. Living at home again was a big mistake. I whispered some words into the metal box, trying to suck power into my voice, knowing how integral it was to not sound weak. *I do not believe it,* I said. He had promised this would never happen in a million years. I reminded him of this. He spoke my name, then. Three syllables with an intake of air. I could not understand how, if he loved me, this could happen.

I will not forgive you, if you do this. The last thing he said was that X believed they could still love one another, that they deserved a try. I walked around my mother's kitchen and couldn't find the fallen phone. I looked at her jar of garlic, the corners already brown and soft.

Evelyn A. So

Bermuda

W hen I was about four or five years old, my family and I visited Bermuda. When I think about that visit, I think of tranquility and rare interludes in which everyone in my family enjoyed each other's company. The first time my parents and sister went to Bermuda, I was too young to travel. From what I've gathered, that was their first major trip since the death of my older brother. At the Princess Hotel, everything seemed to sparkle, from the lobby's counter tops to our bathroom's tiles. Mornings were spent lingering around the breakfast table, which could only mean we were on vacation. A cart and table on wheels appeared at our door, with white tablecloths and trays of scrambled eggs, buttered toast, blueberry muffins, pitchers of freshly squeezed juices, and bowls of pink grapefruit, my favorite. Each half of grapefruit glistened with sugar, topped with a maraschino cherry. When we were full, my sister and I insisted on "feeding the fish," and we stepped onto the balcony and tossed muffin crumbs into the aquamarine water.

Afternoons, the hotel maintained the British custom of serving "high tea," piping hot, with plenty of milk and cream and sugar. At home, we drank tea straight, brewed from Lipton's instant orange pekoe tea bags, or, on special occasions, Chinese tea leaves. Each version was delicious, but nothing like "high tea." Horses appeared with a carriage and a man dressed as Santa outside the hotel on Christmas morning. My sister and I loved our Bermuda T-shirts, pink like everything else at the Princess Hotel. In the buffet line, I became entranced with a Nativity scene of figurines sculpted from butter. It was the first time I had seen butter sculptures, perhaps the first time I had seen a Nativity scene, and I didn't leave until I was satisfied I had memorized their expressions.

Most nights, my sister and I fell asleep soon after we were put to bed, but one night, after our parents had gone downstairs, we were awake. We shared a room on the other side of the door from where our parents slept. A brass lamp hung from the ceiling, and we would pull the cord to turn the lamp on and off. Normally we were well-behaved, but that night, our excitement at being away from home got the better of us, and we giggled and tossed pillows and jumped on the bed. Later that night, or another night, our parents hustled us into the hall. Rarely allowed to stay up past our bedtime, we sat on the carpeted staircase and watched musicians play and elegantly dressed figures dance below, our eyes growing big when we saw our parents among the dancers. That's the only time I saw them dance together.

Nan Friedley

Highway

After midnight work,
Spotlights illuminating
CalTrans nightshifters.

Road hog threading lanes
Claiming freeway real estate
Leave us in his wake.

Corona crawling
Inching rows of red brake lights
Creeping parking lot.

Rose Marie McNair

Serena

In April 1997 I am writing one of my sporadic and random journal entries. The vignette includes my two-year old granddaughter Serena. Here's how it goes: *The first day I write in this journal, I'm with my granddaughter Serena—two-years old on March 24th. Watching her is like seeing some artist's rendition of the perfect world—spring day, a little murky from the rain but the clouds are light and give promise to the sun. She sees a blue jay, tries to creep up on it and the...almost begins to take flight as the bird glides effortlessly out of her reach. Now the black cat, Kato, slips by her and under the fence into the garden. Serena, her golden curls bouncing, runs to the garden gate—"I wanna see Kato," she commands.* I attempt to comply by trying to snatch Kato and I think to myself that my life is now like an off-Broadway play, and I'm just the stage-hand working the props for Director Serena. Kato has grown used to her and patiently allows her to touch his soft fur, but only very briefly before slipping out of her grasp. I watch her like a hawk, as she chases Kato and finds an old truck to push in the dirt. She knows I'm there, and yet she knows I stay just enough behind not to hover over her. I've learned that at two years old, she demands to have her own space. Yet, I also know how sweet and fierce our mutual love is for one another. Even when she is grown, we shall hold a treasured bond—almost psychic and beyond comprehensive reality. Serena and I have become accustomed to these moments together and I am aware of *HER*—of her strong, almost enigmatic persona, her precocious understanding and her sometimes shocking intuitive nature. *"Let's go on a treasure hunt, Roro!"* Our treasure hunts involve the gathering of flowers, like dandelions, some of which, when dried, become 'wishes" we blow. We collect moss attached to fences, rocks and sticks of all shapes and sizes, and once we found a snake's skin that had been shed. She saves them all and we tape and glue them in make-shift scrapbooks that I keep because they are so precious.

The next writing in that same journal takes place in May of 2011, 14 years later: *Michael, my husband has been working on a new start-up. He and his partners have several international patents. I've never been very technically savvy, and even though we've been married 45 years, I have no idea what his "vertical test equipment" does. After the famous dot-com crisis, venture capital virtually dried up. Not only that, Michael's health is now declining rapidly. As a juvenile-onset diabetic, who had lived life to the fullest, his body isn't working properly now. One thing we know for certain, our granddaughter Serena will cheer him up today. We enjoy her so much; we are the proud grandparents who believe she's brilliant. It's just a little after 7:00 pm, as she leaves to go home with her dad. We hug and she looks into her Papa's eyes and says, "You WILL get better, Papa—I just know it."* And he really does seem better...

I never wrote anything more in that journal. My writing has been random and I find notebooks and scraps of paper with things I write to clear my mind, to lift the veil that hides my soul. It surprises me that it's been three years since Michael passed on. I'm writing three paragraphs now about our beloved granddaughter, who is now a sophomore at San Francisco State, and how her sweetness is inter-woven with our lives. Time, so precious, can never be captured or lengthened, yet our memories play before us with so much light and love that I feel like I'm bursting with joy. Come on, Serena, let's find a Dandelion wish and blow on it, so that it reaches Papa.

Amy Mackelden

What is different and what stays the same?

The biggest difference was shoes. And you'd put weight on, which isn't a casual mention or a bitch, but a thing I thought you'd never do. My memory preserved you a certain way. Like cassette tape cases or Clooney. Your shoes I saw first, pretending to look at my phone, waiting for you to round the corner, six years from having seen you.

My sister always made fun of your shoes: Dr. Martens so old the fully fledged hole in the toe let rain in. I loved the way your skinny jeans, bandage tight, sat on the boot cusp. How you dressed I could eat like Christmas cake, from the outside, icing in.

You dress better now: your ex-wife's taste, your Mum's money. No more rough edges, or seam torn t-shirts with Smiths' album prints on. Still, I'm not going to forget. There are moments I will never. I'm glad your metamorphosis was off-camera; I revel in every reveal.

Jane Matchak

Diving for pearls

Woke up watching the sun grace your face. Packed up bag and drove through the honey-glazed hills to southern California. Spent days walking along streets and lying in bed. I remember how your body felt like a sanctuary; dear, I was a refugee. But you remain in southern California and we were only temporary. Drove away with dewy eyes. Woke up watching the sun turn my ivory sheets to butter. But I prefer those honey-glazed hills. And I prefer your softness—smoothing, sweeter than butter; dear, you were marmalade.

Now it's 1:39AM and I'm not sleeping

I haven't slept in five months

Dozing o f f

Cold sweat and everyone in my dream is laughing too laugh

Mama please stop calling

please stop worrying

I'm going to be okay

going to walk around

walk until I find a place that wants me

find that lover with soft sighs

soft side.

I don't know exactly when you'll return. I think I may be losing my mind. I don't know exactly when it'll return. Maybe I will find both in the Lost and Found, among other elusive things. You filled a void that I thought was a vacuum. I'm tired of these friends and these feelings—at least the latter is sincere. And I'm tired of not sleeping, knowing I will not wake up watching the sun grace your face. There's no need to worry; I'll get better one of these days. Just don't tell me to change my ways; I'm a collection of bad habits. Oh dear, I'll wait patiently: drink until my teeth turn to pearls, read until the books catch fire, wake up watching the sun wash my dirty windows. I'll do what's *familiar* to feel *better.*

Three Suits

Y ou've heard the old saying "the clothes make the man"? I'm not so sure it's not the other way around. Consider the estate sale my wife and I attended a few months ago. Estate sales are really glorified garage sales where someone passes away, the family have chosen the heirlooms they want to keep, and they hire an "estate liquidator" to dump the rest. These sales usually last for a weekend or two and prices drop dramatically on the last day before the final items are either donated or tossed. We like to visit estate sales on that last day just in case some precious treasures may have been overlooked and this particular estate held great promise. I was sure I could find something we couldn't live without. There was a lifetime's worth of accumulation from the recently deceased owner. Picture frames and Christmas decorations, old tools and antique furniture, the remnants of a life well lived, all marked at 50% off on this final day. As we made our way into the master bedroom, I spotted an open closet full of clothes that the owner would no longer need. Three suits were hanging in the corner with little tags marked at $3.00. Since this was the final day each suit would cost me $1.50. I had never bought used clothes from one of these estate sales, but $1.50 a suit was too good to pass up. I pulled one of the jackets off the hanger, certain that it would never fit my vertically challenged and stocky frame. It fit perfectly. I took all three suits, paid my $4.50, and walked out convinced I had the bargain of the century. After dry cleaning I moved them into my wardrobe and labeled the suit bags with my twisted sense of humor, DMW, for Dead Man Walking, never considering the man who once wore them.

Three months later I took my 90 year old father and his 89 year old girlfriend on a morning walk down Santana Row, Silicon Valley's answer to Hollywood's Rodeo Drive. It was a fabulous Spring morning and I parked my Toyota in the last parking lot since it didn't fit in well with the Ferraris and Teslas lining the street. My Dad and his girlfriend humored me as we window shopped at stores with prices that cater to the tech gazillionaires who frequent them. Peering in the window of a high end men's store, a brightly colored object caught my eye. It was a beautiful multi-hued bowtie worn by an impeccably dressed mannequin. Having worn conventional neckties for the last 30 years, I had recently switched over to bowties to change things up. This one was perfect. "After all, how much could one bowtie cost?" I asked myself as I walked in the door, my elderly companions in tow. The proprietor, a sharply dressed Afghan gentleman, greeted us at the door. "Come on in… sit down… have some tea… I'm Franco. Your Dad and Mom are so handsome, they remind me of my parents." He didn't let me get a word in edgewise as he proceeded with his pitch. Franco looked me up and down and proclaimed, " Your pants are too baggy, and white shirts are out . Love the shoes though. Have a seat ..let me help you." He quickly grabbed a coat off his rack and held it out for me to try on. What could I do? I glanced down at the sleeve and saw a tag that said 38S. Okay, I thought, $385.00, I can do this. After all it was my birthday in a couple of days and I needed a new suit. Franco brought out some slacks, a shirt, cufflinks and the requisite bowtie. It was too late to turn back. Ten minutes later I walked out, my bank account some $2,000 lighter.

Just a month after the Santana Row excursion, my Dad and I were sitting at my childhood home. He sensed my frustration that my fancy suit wasn't ready yet. It turns out that

Franco had "lost" the original suit and I had to go back in and get measured. Dad was mad and he urged me to cancel the sale. "I have some suits" he said. "I don't wear them anymore. You can cancel the deal and I'll give them to you." And then, the coup de grace. "Mom always picked them out for me. I know they would look great on you." Mom has been gone for twelve years. She died shortly after their 50th anniversary. We went back to his bedroom and he pulled out a beautiful three piece wool suit from his closet. It felt tailor-made for me. I visualized my Mom shopping for this and presenting it to Dad to wear as he visited his patients. "I can't take this Dad, you may need it sometime soon." Dad shook his head and gave me a sad little smile "Tim, the next time I wear a suit will be at my funeral." My dad, the son of penniless immigrants, is the only real hero I have ever had. He worked his way through Stanford University and became one of the first Asian physicians in Santa Clara Valley. He served on a tank in the Battle of the Bulge and never drank and never swore. He paid for all five of his children's college educations and now he was preparing in his mind for the inevitable end by passing on an older suit from his beloved wife. That day I took him out in the garden of the home he had built and had the pool man take a picture of us proudly wearing the suits my mother had chosen many years ago. I know that this is the suit I will cherish above all others, that the value lies not in the cloth but in the man who wore it.

Stranded

He'd cross the ocean:
With long-held breath, salt-soaked bones.
He would if he could.

Wander fathoms deep
'Til seaweed grew around his
Heart—his mind, coral dust.

If he could. If only
He knew there would be someone
On the other shore.

Mary Martine

Three views from the end of a rope

I hate my life, I hate my life, I hate my life! I can't take it anymore. I'm so done! They will never understand. Ever! They put me on pills that make me tired and gain weight and hallucinate. I'm not a guinea pig with all these pills that do nothing to make me feel better. NOTHING!! And the dark swirls tell me I'm worthless and I should just end it. Mom & Dad waste their money on therapists. Five or six and counting. The last two wouldn't even see me after I screamed at them in their waiting rooms and told them how stupid they were and that I wouldn't talk to them. They are idiots! I've hated every one and it doesn't help. Nothing helps! Mom asks what she can do for me and I say "kill me!" I try and she stops me. Today is it.

We went to the house to pick up some stuff and I was trying to talk to Mom. She was looking at me but I could tell she wasn't listening to me, because sissy was having another meltdown. Sissy ran into her room and Mom talked to me for a minute, but as usual, told me she had to check on sissy. I went into my room and started texting my friends because they always text me back and say they are sorry I'm sad, and want to do things to make me happy. Then Mom yelled, "Come quickly! Bring scissors!" She was talking fast and I knew something bad had happened. I ran into the room and Mom was standing on the side of the bed holding onto sissy. I couldn't tell what was happening, and then she told me to climb up and try to cut the belt off sissy's neck while she held onto her. I was really scared sissy was going to die, and I tried but I couldn't cut through all the knots, and I didn't want to accidentally cut her neck. I finally untied it after a few minutes and then we all sat on the bed. Sissy was crying, but calmer, like she always is after she does something to hurt herself. Later, in my support group at school, we all had to tell the worst story of what had happened with our sisters, and I won the prize. It was a candy bar.

Mary Martine

It was too quiet. There was always a calm after the storm, but this storm wasn't over, that much I knew. I don't usually leave her alone when I can tell her mood is dark, despite the screaming that ensues about her needing to be left alone, and the cries of, "Mom, stop invading my space!" It is never wise, the scars on her arms testament to that. I didn't see her when I walked in but she didn't usually hide. I walked to the other side of her canopy bed and will never forget the terror of that moment, and confronting something so horribly close to my worst fear. She was standing on the footboard with one end of the dress belt tied to the top of the canopy and the other around her neck, her face turning pink. All she had to do to hang herself was step down, her previous "cries for help" dress rehearsals for this moment, which with one little slip could have been her final act. My younger one and I worked frantically, speaking in hushed, quick, sparse words until we freed her, and then we all gulped air in quick bursts, as if we'd run a race. After we got her down, with our hearts beating normally again, I held her, all three of us silent. She sobbed quietly, her despair palpable and intense, as if carried from several lifetimes of heartache. These hardships she endures come from within, a mental torment, difficult to ward off and striking randomly. I never feel like I say the right things. What is the right thing to say? "I'm sorry for this pain you must endure? I'm sorry you were born with this mental illness?" Words seem so trite when dealing with the gravity of

70

THREE

these incidents, her despair, the guilt and heartache I bear for my inability to find her the help she needs or provide any kind of normal life for either of my children; the helplessness I feel seeing her suffer, with no way to make it better. Time has been the only salve, to wait, listening to her sorrow and despondency until it passes. The ensuing calm is always sweet, brief respite to be savored and appreciated. For one thing is always certain. The shadow will descend again, and I will watch my child disappear into the darkness of her illness.

Remembering

With my knees bent and feet dug into the sand, I held my arms out above my head and braced myself. I taunted and begged that big stupid rock above me to fall piece by piece so that I could smooth and rebuild its jaded surface. Alas, the rock began to crumble and the edifice I planned was strong in my mind. But soon, pebbles turned into boulders, and I found myself hit by the full blow of one of their impacts. Bruised, I walked aimlessly around the remains of this mighty boulder as my fingertips grazed its sharp jagged edges. I leaned against its cold exterior and watched the sun set along the ocean's horizon, as I pondered the depth of the water's blue abyss, the magnitude of its waves, and the wealth of its hues. I looked around to see my cliff lying in pieces around me, dilapidated in structure and unrecognizable in character. I tried moving each of them; I lifted and pushed, to no avail. Instead, they sunk deeper and deeper into the sand and became immobile. Without hope, I stepped over pebbles and shards and sank my weathered hands and feet into the ocean, allowing its salt to clean my open wounds. It stung refreshingly and I yearned to be fully submerged in something so vast and unknown. I took a deep breath, dunked my head under, and glided beneath the surface. The lack of clarity around me was calming as I explored in every direction. One curiosity after another brought me further and further away from the start as the ocean and the sky slowly swallowed the outline of the shore. After a while I became exhausted. I raised my legs and floated, letting the sun permeate my skin and trusting the waves to bring me to land again. That night I went to sleep in London praying that I could remember one last time.

And there he was in the distance, in a familiar stance, with a familiar smile, and a familiar laugh. At an average height, with a slender build, he stood slightly leaned in, genuinely acknowledging every person around him. All I saw was his dusty brown hair, his green eyes, and his scarred pale skin. His eyes met mine and he looked down. Disappointment seeped through his gentle physic. As he slowly came nearer his head titled, eyebrows rose, forehead wrinkled, mouth frowned, and lips pressed tightly together. I knew he was not happy to see me. His gait was lackadaisical but his eyes were purposeful and locked on mine. He came to stand before me and with his eyes he filled my body with warmth. I let every ounce of his poison saturate my limbs and I felt high. He smiled, and I knew he had been expecting me. I couldn't move or say anything and what seemed like for the first time, I could just be. There were moments in that dream where I swear to God I felt him behind me with his scruffy cheek pressed against my ear, his lips slowly making their way across my face until they finally met mine. Everything around us became a dream, leaving our connection the only reality we found true. And in a moment, it was gone.

That morning, I awoke in Paris at Pont des Arts. I stood with my hands tightly gripping the cold black iron bars of a bridge suspended over the Seine. The extremes of my peripheral vision were filled with hundreds of locks of all shapes, sizes, and colors. One of them reads BP+BG and it tells the story of a sad love and two people who were trapped inside of it. This love was as heavy as a mountain of rocks, and even with an ocean between us I could not set it down because no place and no one was worthy of its beauty. But I was tired and worn. I reached into my pocket and took out the three keys and began to slowly unwind one off their ring. I held it in my palm and I clenched my fist so tight that my nails began to dig into my skin. I brought the key to my lips, kissed it, and whispered; "I'm locking you away, here, so that I know where I can always find you." With my head bowed I slowly extended my arms beyond the railing and let the key fall from my grasp. My vision tunneled as I watched the key fall towards the muddy waters and an avalanche of panic materialized before my eyes. With a gentle plop, the key penetrated the brownish waters and I looked up at the murky sky to find solace in what epitomized the chaos of my emotions. Then, in an instant, time seemed to start moving faster and faster. With nothing left to say or do, I paid my respects to my love, my loss, and my dignity. Then, I turned around and walked away.

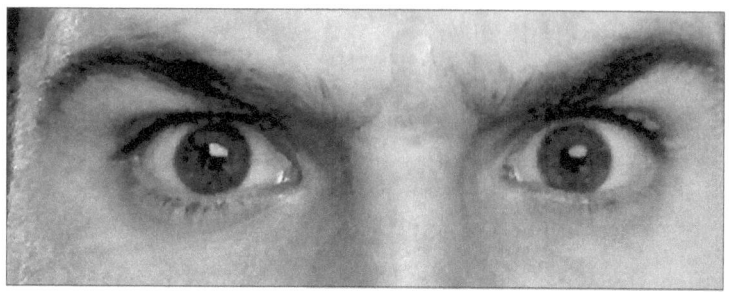

The angle of my eyes

They were oh so round.
Both of ours were, a perfect match.
Glowing eyes, young love.

Last kiss, I didn't know.
Your life then came to an end,
Along with our glow

I am not angry,
but whichever emotion,
round is now a slant

Daniel Wallock

The heart monitor beeps

The heart monitor beeped. The air was as thick as the blood that had crusted over the white sheets next to my chest. Yesterday was the last day I would breathe, or that's what I thought. I thought that my life would be gone. All perception faded as the nurse counted down those horrible numbers. I had debated suicide and even attempted it before the surgery, but this was the closest I had come to dying.

The bed would never be a home. The bed held my tattered flesh and rippled blood. The doctors told me that I had lost a dangerous amount of blood. My parents stood horrified remarking that I was whiter then a ghost. It seemed that all was distant. I was distant. The needles only spent a few days penetrating the flesh in my arms. Meanwhile, the moments of the hospital stuck with me forever. They were still images and moving feelings. I will never forget when the chest tubes were yanked from my body. The tubes creased and jolted each organ as they swiveled inside of me.

All is beautiful in tragedy. Beaming down on my back the sun brought me light. Sitting in the wheelchair the California breeze brushed my face. The blue sky, clear air, and the sweet noise of the young birds. Tears slipped down my face. My fingers shook and my eyes blinked, capturing not just an image, but a feeling. I was free.

Thomas Leikam

Prelude

sweet impossible taste
peach juice dripping down your body
ecstasy unleashed

in night's slumber
swans drift elegantly by
in perfect harmony

impossibilities
sweetness drenching the soul
opening death's door

Tess Crescini

In between dreams

In between dreams where identities are negotiated, modified, and sometimes transformed, I struggle to wake to find the Self who won the wrestling match with the multiple personalities that wrangle with each other for dominance. In my waking reality, I need to be on time to a place I don't want to be, but need to be... with my 80-year-old father at Modesto General Hospital to watch the poking; prodding for a vein; for the blood-letting into tubes and more tubes; to be there for the insertion of catheter in his penis; for the liver biopsy; for the draining of fluids from his lower gastrointestinal tract only to be caught up in the waiting. Waiting for the laboratory results which can confirm or deny how much time we have to learn to die; how much time before we start to rot like the meat we are... definitely not the stuff dreams are made of... Spirit informing the Eternal with patterns of the collective, the spirals, the circles, the Alpha and the Omega; a Being of existing reality—all the phenomenon of being human.

Then there's my mother. Like Alice in Wonderland who ate something that made her small, drowning in her own tears, tumbles in the flowing waters, fights with the cross currents not of her choosing to hold on to me. I have become a tree rooted to the ground of my being, tapping into my inner world for strength before the underworld abducts me, too. I am strong and silent. My dying father says to me he dreamt he was lying down in his mother's lap. She was rubbing his head, saying, "*kasi ang tigas ng ulo mo, eh*" (because you are so hard headed). He did not want to give up his cigarettes, his San Miguel beers, and the *lechon kawali* that he was told would kill him. To those naysayers, he would retort, "We're all going to die; I might as well enjoy the ride while I can." My father is no philosopher, but I think he grasped Kierkegaard's quote, "Life can only be understood backwards, but it must be lived forwards."

In between the living and the dying, my parents' home became a hospice, a place for at-tending to the emotional and spiritual needs of the family. But hospice also came to mean not much time left; cancer is in the liver, in the thyroids, in the lower intestine, everywhere like a wrathful god, shifting the room around as the usual relationship patterns enter a crucible where they are heated and stressed; where sometimes cracks are made visible at the weak bonds forged by anger and regrets, but sometimes, beautiful shapes appear burnished by the difficulty to reveal unexpected rich moments of tenderness and forgiveness. Then my father took his last breath. In my dreams, I am the great Inanna, the Sumerian goddess of writing, fertility, and warfare, who descends to the underworld to be with her sister, Ereshgikal, only to find herself stripped naked, hung on a meat hook to die, decomposes into a green mass who with one drop of the water of life on her blue lips arose from the great below to return to the great above.

Christopher Danaher

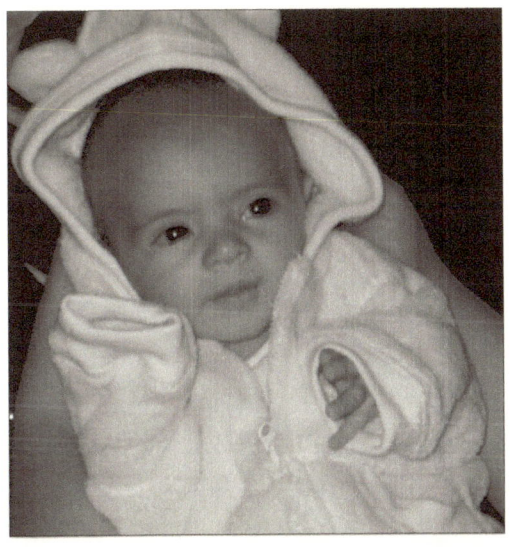

Ecstasy

sweet little smile—
not just the empty pipe
dreams of a broken man;

those innocent eyes—
green, deeper than any bottle:
pick me up;

invitation to live,
to know when to quit—
again, daddy, again

My father's golf clubs

My father's golf clubs are tucked away in my attic, beside the old paint cans and beach chairs and umbrellas. He carried these clubs on the day he died playing golf almost 20 years ago now. After his death, my stepmother gave the clubs to my uncle, who years later gave them to me. And then when my wife and I moved into our home a decade ago, I set them in a corner of the attic. I've only used them one time since then.

Every once in a while, always while searching for something else, I spot the golf clubs. I may even pull out his rust-specked putter or the seven-wood with the cracked rubber grip, squeeze it in my hands and imagine him playing his final round. I wonder if he played well that day, if he was under or over par. These are the sorts of things you don't think about until later, much later.

While the clubs may not be predominantly displayed, still there's something about having them close by that I find comforting. My father was not a man prone to sentimentality and would probably tell me to sell them for fifty bucks if I wasn't going to use them. But I have no intention of doing that. They were the last things he touched before leaving this world, and I'm still not ready to let go of them or of him.

Eye-level

We spotted each other from a distance. Large blue-black eyes, unblinking, stared at me from underneath a dirty mop of brown and off-white. It was like he singled me out, zeroing in on me through the collective yet unconcerned gaze of the others. As I took a few anxious steps forward, he pushed the others out of his way, bullying the slightly shorter, dirtier, weaker ones. My heart was pounding, but I had somehow become a paperclip to which he was a behemoth magnet. He was moving closer and, against all instincts, I was being pulled forward as well. He stopped at the wooden fence that divided us, his large sinister eyes bearing down on me. For some reason the field suddenly became hushed, as if everyone was anticipating my next move. I gulped and unceremoniously stared back. A large, pointed beak protruded from his face just beneath the furrows of his brow. A look of severe contempt sat indignantly on his face. I glanced at the others, and noticed they all bore the same fierce expression. There was no turning back now, the crowd of nine-foot-tall, ebony-feathered birds was waiting to eat. I swallowed again, and brought up my long arms, grasping the small tray of bird feed with both hands outstretched. As I attempted to lengthen my arms and keep my feet planted as far back from the fence as possible, the ostrich who had "chosen" me brought down his beak, opening it large enough to reveal a long row of tiny shark-like teeth lining the jaw, and pecked vigorously at the feed. I had not anticipated such force and almost lost my grip on the bird feed twice. My initial fears of being picked apart, gave way to cooling beads of sweat on my forehead. I took another step forward, albeit gingerly. The other ostriches, as if suddenly realizing they were missing out, began pushing and shoving their way to the front of the line. The most aggressive ones began to bob their own heads down towards the bin of feed in my delicate hands. As each ostrich poked and prodded the feed-bucket, the pellets flew into the air and onto the ground. In my adrenaline-induced state, I barely heard my son repeatedly chiding me on the supreme wastage of food that was occurring at my hands.

Most people went on vacations to relax by the beach, or visit exotic street markets, often drinking from the cup of luxury. My family always wound up at the most bizarre and unheard of locations; somewhere like Solvang, a quaint little Danish town north of Santa Barbara. TripAdvisor reviewers claimed Solvang would take us to Denmark in the middle of the vast, green central California hills. Yet somehow we managed to miss the butter cookies and windmills and, instead, discovered the frightfully interesting Ostrich Land: a haven for Ostrich-lovers and freaks alike. The concept of Ostrich Land was simple: you came to Ostrich Land, bought the ostrich feed (one dollar per shovel of pellets), attempted to feed the birds, failed and had your husband do it instead while you took pictures and the kids squealed in semi-nervous delight. I remember thinking how monumental it would be to show the kids these magnificent creatures up close. Having always been dreadfully ornithophobic, however, I had done my research on the overall safety of the place. Thankfully, most Yelp reviews claimed that the entire ostrich-feeding experience was mostly just creepy. Furthermore, none of the reviews even minutely indicated any incidents of mild-decapitation or loss-of-life.

When there were no more pellets left, I took a couple steps back to signal to the ostriches that lunchtime had ended. Most ostriches knew to walk away at this juncture in our short encounter, but a couple of them stayed, mimicking my own curiosity towards them. Even before I had reached my own full stature of 5 feet and 11.5 inches tall, I had grown accustomed to the isolation that it imparted on me. Back in grade school, I had never been able to link arms with my girlfriends. I had towered a couple feet above my friends, and holding hands had been a physical impossibility. I could push my shorter, lighter counterparts on the tire-swing, but no one was ever willing to return the favor. There were other repercussions of being "tall for my age." Many thought I had flunked elementary school, others thought I was slow. My own parents and teachers, however unconsciously, expected more from me because I looked older than my true age. In fifth grade, I remember trying to will my body to stop growing altogether. I had not understood nor accepted what was the fabric of my core. As a 29-year-old Pakistani Muslim who struggles to succeed—as mom, wife, student, amateur chef, and writer—there are days when I want to stick my own head into the ground. But even ostriches don't actually do so, not even when they are afraid. Perhaps they've known all along what has taken me three decades to comprehend. I have accepted the person I was once, and the individual that I am today. In our final moments together, I let myself absorb our shared space, viewing the ostriches in a wholly different light. I looked at them with a profound and unusual clarity. We were creatures of immense height, bound by a dignified and solemn fate. It wasn't a curse, or an impediment. It was a mutual solitude. We were equals. We stood, at last, eye-to-eye.

Acting up in Italy

My love for Vienna had not waned, but my Viennese lover's love for me had. I packed my rucksack and took the first train south for the sun, warmth, and friendly souls of Italy. Little did I know when I purchased my ticket that the train was the happy-go-lucky local, and it stopped at every station. When we finally arrived in San Candito, Italy, it stopped for the night.

Could I sleep on the train? No. So I walked up a steep hill from the station to a stately hotel where the manager informed me that the rooms were $150 (US) and they were booked solid. "But," he said smiling and pointing at my rucksack, "I do have a place for you." With that he led me out onto a spacious veranda with a spectacular view of the Dolomites and pointing to a swath of grass, he said, "Pitch your tent there. Best room in the house. It's free." I set up and joined the other guests at a superb six-course meal served in a spacious room with tables at one end and a bar across the length of the other, both with that same Dolomites view.

After dinner I was standing at the bar when a fellow guest asked me what I did in America. "Corporate America Drop-

Out" was too hard to translate so I chose *rappresentazione*, acting. That, and movie acting in films about cowboys. The man asked me to offer a small scene. He announced loudly to the diners and fellow bar mates that the American would now show some of his acting skill. I got the bartender to set a shot glass full of grappa on the bar, walked to the nearest doorway turned and in pantomime opened and walked through saloon doors. I twirled imaginary six-guns as I walked towards the bar. Once there, I downed the shot, wheeled around, started firing away and was hit twice before slumping to the floor and wriggling twice before dying. A roar of approval went up. I couldn't buy a drink that night and slept peacefully in the shadows of Il Dolomiti.

Erica Goss

Three years gone

thoughts of my father
sorrow is today's teacher
nothing in the mail

low winter sunlight
shadow separates the hills
seam between two worlds

this absence of leaves
my father needed winter
a fresh piece of sky

Morris

My grandmother found an orange Tabby in the backyard of the complex where the elderly Jewish people lived. She named him "Morris" after his 9-Lives namesake. His foraging days over, Morris lived quite regally, often reclining on the chaise lounge my grandmother formerly designated for her boyfriend only. Dad reported on the growing bond between whining old woman and fawning beast during one of our weekly phone calls while I was off at college: "I've never seen anything like it. She loves that cat. He's all she talks about, and he's so loyal to her, follows her all around the apartment."

I thought Dad was a bit jealous since for all the years I had been around, Dad was my grandmother's most faithful worshipper. From experience, I also could have told Morris not to trust the love of a woman who rejected the present I gave her the year before: a 45 rpm version of The Fifth Dimension's "Never My Love" which she said didn't "play right" on the beaten-down phonograph in her living room closet. It was the needle on that ancient player, however, that was faulty, not the record. But then, nothing my grandmother had or did was faulty. It was never her fault. Never her love.

I could have told Morris that my grandmother's love was entirely random and fleeting. But before I could arrive home from college that summer to do so, Morris bit my grandmother, apparently for no reason. And for his trouble, she sent him, still licking his lips, to his new bedroom at the pound without any dinner. "She had to get rid of him," Dad said. "He might have had rabies." But I doubt that. For in that relationship, and with many others, it was my grandmother who was truly mad, though it was the rest of us who had to suffer.

Jessica Sauceda

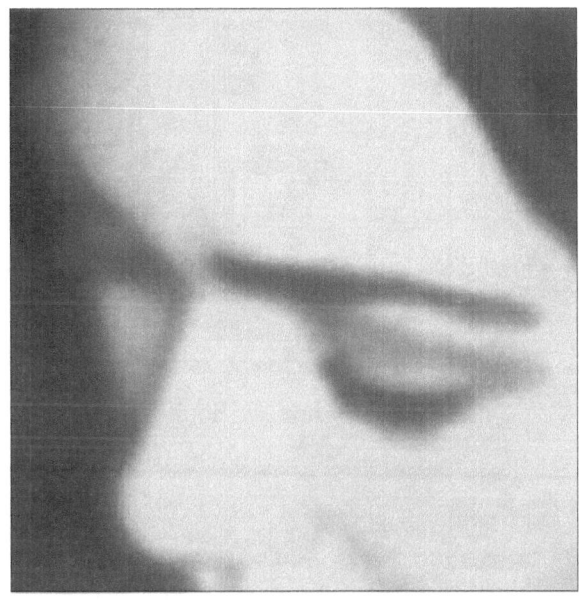

Fragment

Drunken breathing came
With creaking, down the hallway.
My limbs paused mid-stretch.

A marble statue
Frozen, anticipating
An unwelcomed hand.

The smell still lingers.
A cocktail of broken
Time and innocence.

Granite

Three days ago we came here, to Stanford Hospital. The Lucille Packard Children's Hospital, to be precise. There was a birth, a first-born son, Erik, in Santa Cruz. He was fine, then an hour later he wasn't, and streptococcus, contracted during birth, began to ravage his entire biology. His mother and I signed emergency forms. Erik was to be flown to Stanford, then he was too critical to be flown, so they put him in a special ambulance. The ambulance had to pull over once because they thought they were going to lose him there and then. In the meantime, a friendly nurse offered to drive us up; it became the most god-awful one-hour ride of my life. A harrowing nighttime drive over Highway 17 and its treacherous curves consumed our nerves, the heavy blackness rising before us, barely pierced by the meager headlights of the old Volkswagen. We drove along a thinly lit tunnel through an ever-encompassing nightmare, then suddenly the hospital was in front of us. I was in scrubs. My wife was in scrubs. Erik lay on a table, helpless and plugged into everything, on his back, eyes closed and crying silently. He was beautiful. Above his head, on a wall-mounted chart, the medical stickers began multiplying.

Each one added to the dry, precise record of what we were to be charged for. The nurses started a second chart to collect them all. Erik lay helpless and was beautiful, and when I spoke and sang to him his heart rate elevated. He knew me, I am certain of that. Don't argue with me; he knew who I was.

I looked up. We never left. Years passed, and he was the same age. I watched him through it all, except for going to the bathroom and stepping into a side room to eat whatever food family and friends had brought for us. My wife left the hospital in the tender care of my aunt and uncle. She was broken, and so was I, but "resting" was not a word I could hear. Then she was there in front of me, back from an extended caretaking visit to my relatives' home, and when I couldn't hear her speaking to me, I realized I was gone. I went reluctantly and excruciatingly to my aunt and uncle's house. Sitting at their beautiful, polished Italian granite counter top, I ate my Chinese comfort food slowly, without taste or solace. Slowly, slowly neither soup nor noodles nor tea brought any relief from the heavy stones in my belly. I stared, dumbfounded. The phone rang. Surprisingly, it was a rather plain phone, almost out of place in this ultra-beautiful home, except for its color, which complemented the granite's hue. My wife's voice: "CAT scan shows very little activity; extremities turning blue, erratic everything." A final decision was made, but not to be enacted until I returned to the hospital: Erik's time had come. We would disconnect him, untying him from this world, and hold him as if our lives were nothing and his was everything. I felt intellectually safe, but emotionally eviscerated, as if life would not ever fully return to me in a recognizable form.

We chose granite for Erik's tiny gravestone. It was polished, and though it wasn't from Italy, it was the same color as my uncle's kitchen granite. I know. I looked at it long enough.

Jesse Mardian

Accidents

Don't be mad, he tells me, you are old enough to know. These things happen all the time. Waves crash in the distance. The fire cracks and sparks flurry upwards like lightning bugs. His eyes glisten in the orange glow and he sips the whiskey from a coffee mug. A smell of seaweed lingers in the smoky air. Our tents stand still on the beach.

Like a fishing pole, I dangle a straightened coat hanger into the fire. At its end, a marshmallow darkens. Maybe that wasn't the right word, he says. Miracle, that's it! You were a miracle. He is happy with himself now. He hugs me. His stubble braises my cheek. It feels like grip tape. His fiery breath meets my nape and then he pulls away.

Don't get tight, Junior, he tells me. Hear that? The swell is picking up. Just forget I said it. It doesn't really matter now does it? From the fire, I raise the coat hanger. The mallow is like charcoal. The once white sweetness, gone. I contemplate keeping it as it begins to slide off the metal. There are so many more in the bag. It would be easy to start anew. Best get rid of it, he says while staring at the sticky morsel seeping. Before it is too late, I wedge the mallow in between the two graham crackers and take a bite. Even charred it's still good.

Jane Matchak

Serotonin

Your words are sincere
When I'm scratching at my skin;
we make a nice pair.

I think about us
living together with glass
windows and skimmed books.

I'm getting better;
I can't even explain how
good you are for me.

Yasmin Ramirez

Dimming lights

Through the screen door in the living room, I saw the burnt-orange desert light hover low on the mountain horizon. I stood in the hallway shadows and watched my mom rock back and forth, creaking, in a brown wooden rocking chair. The chair, with faded paisley cream accents on the back, had been around longer than I had been alive, the creaking, a loud metronome in the sudden silence of the Javier Solis CD stopping. The radio emitted a low electronic hum, the imprint from his voice heavy in the air. A tangible emptiness, the rocking only punctuated with each creak.

I came to change the CD, to mask the heavy silence coating everything in the house, where I'd been raised, in the days since my Ita died; now I was stuck, feet anchored to the worn wooden floor. She hadn't seen me, and in truth I didn't want her to. I held my breath, wishing that I'd walked toward the room from the dining room or that the worn wooden floors had creaked a little louder. I looked up, thankful for the dim dusk light, then toward the darkened hallway. I envisioned tip-toeing back on the balls of my feet, step by step. I glanced back and saw my mom's face again, caught, enthralled in a scene I wished I wasn't witnessing.

My mom hugged my sleeping niece, Mica, to her chest, a life preserver in a pool into which she was sinking. She stared into the nothingness in front of her, the light deepening from burnt orange to indigo, illuminating dust motes finishing their last dance. My jaw clenched as I tried to swallow everything I saw, my mom's face, always bright and ready for a fight, now hollowed and pale, drawn in on itself. She looked up into the darkening night, her deep-set eyes matching the dimming of the room.

Amor fati

I caught you cheating when she returned your letter. A catastrophe hid inside. I tied our room around my waist with a thick, old rope and I carried it with me when I left. The fall ached so, the air like a dull razor against bare skin as I pulled us through the mud. Each time I stopped to catch my breath, a litter of dead leaves gathered at my feet. Heavily pregnant with the giant box of our things, I trudged the backroads to find answers.

Mostly I was alone with the trees. Going downhill was not safe; I had to cross the cornfields at a wide angle to avoid everything toppling over. It took a long time. At night, I parked our room like a house in town and went inside to sleep on your correspondence. I opened and reread everything in case there was something new. There were sentiments there I could pretend were for me. There were responses I said aloud in my own voice.

I moved our room and our things and your letters each day to new places. Once, I saw a woman outside raking. When I showed her the letters and told her your name, she raised her hand to stop me. She said angrily, "Don't wage war on ugly."

It was the fall that ached so, a handful of old letters on the ground. I didn't understand but I embraced it. Ultimately, you had turned away even when I whispered – "yes."

Susan Forrest

Mother's best Christmas

O ur mother was beautiful. Drop-dead beautiful, according to our aunts and uncles—part Katherine Hepburn, part Gene Tierney. By the time she reached eighteen, they told us, people would turn and gape as she passed. Mother (as we called her) had an air of sophistication about her that implied wealth and status. But we were far from wealthy. Daddy worked as a baker and Mother was a legal secretary.

Woolworth's doors flew open at 9:00AM on December 24th, 1960. Daddy ushered us into the entrance. For the first time ever, my sister, Janet, and I had saved enough allowance buy Mother a Christmas present with our own money. Daddy gave us a half hour to choose our gift, threw in an extra seventy-five cents, then hurried across the street to buy Mother a fully-fashioned Ban-lon sweater. Janet and I knew exactly what we wanted to buy there. Months before, while our parents had shopped at Woolworth's, Janet and I wandered off and became captivated by an exquisite Evening in Paris midnight-blue bottle. The salesgirl sprayed some in the air for us to sniff. We swooned. So on December 24th, we raced through the store, almost knocking over a stooped old man who'd just finished sweeping dust into a big pile near the perfume stand where a sales lady was setting up her display. She opened a silver box lined with lush white satin. Inside, beckoning us, nestled a cobalt blue bottle of Evening in Paris cologne, a fancy flask of perfume, and an embossed tin of talcum powder. We gasped. This would last Mother for months! The sales lady asked if she could help. Certain we could never afford such a treasure, I tried to croak out a question, but nothing came out. I turned to Janet. She just stood there, eyes glued to the gift box. As her more responsible seven-year-old sister, I took charge and stood tall. "Um... well... how much is this one?" I asked. "Three dollars and twenty-five cents," said the sales lady.

Janet and I scooped pennies, dimes, nickels and quarters out of our pockets and dumped them on the counter. Even with Daddy's contribution, I was sure we wouldn't make it. I crossed my fingers behind my back and wished hard. The nice lady counted the coins. "I'm so sorry. You're seventy-five cents short." She gathered up our money and handed it back to me. "Perhaps you'd like something else?" We peered into the display counter at other colognes and perfumes, all dreary in comparison to the dazzling gift box. Fighting back tears, I led Janet away from the counter. Suddenly she froze and pointed, "Look! Over there." A crisp new dollar bill lay on top of the pile of sweepings. "Let's take it," said Janet, "We can buy the present." I refused. "That's stealing." Then we noticed that the old man had disappeared. The sales lady was busily polishing her counter. "Nobody's watching," said Janet. "If we don't take it, that dollar is garbage." She was smart for a five-year-old! I snatched up the dollar and took it back to the sales lady. She wrapped the box, eased it into a Woolworth's Christmas bag, handed it to me, and chirped, "Merry Christmas, girls!"

Kylie Kenner

Frenchy baby (for Louise)

sit by the canal
roll more tobacco, spoon out
more instant coffee

you explain old art
and lingerie, I take notes
how to be like Lou

au revoir, chéri
tears pooled five years ago—I
carry you with me

Linda Lee Ortiz Hughes Bakke

Midas torch 1974

G uam is a lush and sultry nursery where kids rove ferally and reacquaint themselves with the magic cryptographically woven deep within the fiber of a blanketing mirage. We are barefoot without memory of the purpose of shoes; we have curious states of sun bleached hair some deep browns gone orangutan orange. The toe-headed blonde kid's hair has turned to vaporous halos. We would have cared not to be swathed at all as we ran wildly sucking in heavy humid air heady with the compost of the boonies. Today I am left to construct a day on my own. My little gal pal isn't coming by today for my bike-riding lesson, if you can call it that. There is a large cable spool left in our yard by some utility company, large enough to be repurposed as a picnic table, or so my mother devised. My mother wants to paint it. We have, as it so happens and as every household should, a gallon can of lead-based gold metallic paint. I don't have to do much to convince my mother to let me paint the spool. The day is unfolding before me in shimmering strokes of gold paint. Opaque gold covers the ugly knots and raw pine of the spool and my skin. I shout when I am finished anticipating praise as my mother emerges from the cool of our cinder block duplex. She gives me that look like I have let her down and proven her worst fears. I am the sweet, cute, and abiding fawn of her fantasy who has suddenly flashed a fierce muzzle of menacing canines. Her mouth is clamped shut in a thin line that hisses when she attempts to speak, like a valve under pressure. I am covered in enough gold paint that she has to think about it for a moment before grabbing me by a paint free patch on my arm and dragging me over to the patio. Committed still to the idea that I have done a fine job, I gesture coyly back toward my glittering spool-cum-picnic table.

On the patio my mother picks up a can of gasoline. She grabs a rag and starts to douse it with the gas. The sight of it tips me into a panic. Within her grasp I skitter and swing side to side and manage once to spin us 360^0 but I am still unable to wrench free. I slacken, my battered momentum dissolves into blacktop stillness. She pulls me closer and starts to wipe the paint roughly from my skin. Gasoline fumes, threatening permanent damage to my olfactory senses, spark a flash of imagistic montages strewn with bulky stunt men, ablaze, running in slow motion across the scrub of studio back lots, "Don't let Daddy come out here with his cigarette!" She is silent, removing the paint in harsh exfoliating strokes. My short breaths are permeated with gasoline fumes and I spy him, my dad. He is at the kitchen window peering out from the curtains, holding up a cigarette and drawing on it hard so that the cherry ember emanates through the bright glare of the window. I can see his shoulders shaking, he is laughing so hard. "Daddy!" I shriek. My mother is still firmly clamped as she keeps at the business of removing the gold plate. "Lindaaaa…" My dad taunts. "Lindaaa…" "Jackie, Yo-bo!" My mom chides, which just makes him laugh harder. Worse yet, I can see that she is doing her best to keep from laughing also. Panic flares within me and I start to sputter and sob in an incoherent stream of "Daddy don'ts, cigarette, I'm gonna be on fire…" While wildly working to jack free from my mother.

My gasoline-slicked arm finally slides free and I stagger a few feet away from her. I am gutted, standing, in hysterics. My dad comes out with his Cheshire mask barely covering the appearance of his horns. The belly that my mother has already grown on him with midday meals of porterhouse steaks, priced at near nothing from the Navy commissary, jounces with laughter. My mother is still on her knees, gas rag still in hand, laughing and chiding, wiping away a tear and trying to beckon me over all at once. My trust in them is shallow and yet I move toward them hoping to be soothed. I see my mother's face twist in horror before my outstretched hand can reach her—in my mind's eye, I have already burst into flames.

Carlos Barron

Infixed expletives

C an I just twist your ear about something? So don't tell anyone, but between you and me, I think I loved her. It sounds a little ridiculous, I know, but there was always something there. We were friends from the beginning, almost as if we'd been friends in some other far off time and place. I couldn't tell you how it all started. I don't remember how it all started, at least not all of it. I don't remember who caught whose attention, whether I said something sarcastic and she laughed, or whether she said something intelligent and I just happened to notice. I can't tell you how we ended up going to our respective lockers together, or whose idea it was to link arms and literally skip down the hallways, only stopping on account of our backpacks. (We both hated how running with a backpack on made you feel stupid, let alone skipping.) I can't tell you how many times I wished we could spend time together outside of school and extracurriculars. I can't tell you how many times she corrected my grammar and how many times I just corrected her. I can't list all the things that made her amazing, but I can tell you a few of my favorites, like: She once taught me what an infixed expletive was. ("I just hate how he's so up-fucking-tight." "Up-fucking-tight? Can you really call yourself a grammar goddess if you go around butchering words and sewing them back together with cuss words." "Yes, jackass. That's called an infixed expletive, and it's a perfectly acceptable bit of grammar when used for emphasis.") I swear I felt my eyes dilate when she told me that. Her mind was just as attractive as the rest of her...

She loved orange juice more than I did. I even made a habit of giving her the juice I got with my free lunch pass, handing it over during fifth period. I don't think she could have loved the stuff more if it were laced with methyl benzoylecgonine and alpha-hypophamine. Uh, that's crack and oxytocin (the love hormone), on the off chance you didn't know. Anyway, I know she loved the stuff, but it probably wasn't so much the "made from concentrate" crap I gave her that made her smile. I like to think it was the fact that I was thinking of her when I saved it... She never gave me any crap for not dancing at her parties. I danced, just not in public. My self-consciousness didn't do me any favors back then either, but she never said anything about it. She just smiled, and I always got an invitation... She bragged about me to her friends. I'm pretty sure the entire school knew about the necklace I made her, and all the effort that went into it: finding the right shade of red, the right type of bead, stainless steel spacers, and learning how to attach a clasp, etc. She loved that I incorporated metal into the design. Her fashion sense, and her body, allowed her to wear steel-toed boots with a polka dot dress…There were days when she had the audacity to be her beautiful, bright, self even though everything else had decided it was going to be dim and ugly and broken. She was something else entirely, and not the teachers being assholes or the shows she was in getting canceled ever took the song out of her walk …There was no such thing as an awkward silence between the two of us. Tarantino was right. I had found somebody special because I could shut the fuck up and just enjoy the silence…

What do you mean what happened? Life did. She found someone, graduated, moved an hour away, got married, had her happily ever after. We lost touch, and one day she decided I wasn't necessary. To tell you the truth, I can't say I blame her… The night our friendship ended, I happened to have some orange juice in my fridge. So I drank my orange-fucking-juice, and it was good, but would never be as sweet.

Tonya McQuade

Saying goodbye

The tears didn't start falling until we pulled away. That last grasping hug, that last look into his slightly panic-stricken eyes, that last whispered "I love you" … I tried to hold it together as I walked to the car, watching as he pondered where to go next in the crowd of other incoming college freshmen, but once my husband started the engine and we pulled out of the parking lot, my stomach lurched. I swallowed hard, and then the tears started flowing … not only as I thought of the significance of saying goodbye to my first-born as he embarks on a new life, but also as I remembered the feeling of overwhelming loss and panic as I watched my parents drive away from my freshmen dorm on that first day so long ago.

Are we ever fully ready to let our first child go? Or to watch our parents drive away? Sure, I know what the Dalai Lama has said: "Give the ones you love wings to fly, roots to come back and reasons to stay." But it sure is hard to let them take that first solo flight, trusting that we have given them the "wings" they need to soar to success all on their own, to succeed without our "helicopter parenting" keeping them afloat.

Have I done enough? Too much? Have I rescued too often, or have I, rather, provided the roots to ground him for life's trials and difficulties which are sure to come? The roots to stand tall despite failures and losses? Given the choice, have I instilled in my son the "reasons to stay" that will allow him to go out on his own, chasing after his own dreams, yet always desire to eventually find his way back home?

Long ago, awakened by my unborn son's kicking in the middle of the night, I wrote a poem that still hangs on my living room wall:

New Life
A twitch, a flutter, a kick –
each one assures me you are inside,
alive and strong and growing –
a bud soaking in the sunshine
that will cause you to bloom
into full maturity;
a wave gathering strength
as you prepare to break
upon the shores of life;
a rain drop gently falling to earth,
inevitably to join with the pools of humanity;
a baby tenderly being knit together
in your mother's womb –

a mother eagerly and anxiously awaiting

the sound of your cries,

the thrill of your touch,

the warmth of your embrace,

and the joy of your love.

Well, my bud has grown into a mature young flower; my wave is finding his own shore on which to break; my raindrop is joining with the pools of humanity in his quest to find his own path and create his own future. For eighteen years I've experienced his cries, his touch, his embrace, and his love, all in turn filling my heart and mind with memories, laughter, joy, and yes, tears. They've all been a part of this growing up process and are now a big part of the "saying goodbye" as he moves on to a "new life" of his own. I hope his wings will take him far, that his roots will give him strength, and that he will always find reasons to stay … to stay in touch, to stay grounded, to stay hopeful, to stay faithful, and to stay connected to those who love him.

Kate Evans

Infinity

TELL ME, WHAT IT IS YOU PLAN TO DO

WITH YOUR ONE WILD AND PRECIOUS LIFE?

- MARY OLIVER

In our fifties, my husband Dave and I swept aside security to become nomads. After taking a boat down river in Brisbane, after holding a koala, after watching kangaroos box on a beach at sunrise, after snorkeling through a school of squid in the Great Barrier Reef, after hiking the oldest rainforest on earth, I woke one morning in a friends' seaside cottage, a seizure gripping my body. Diagnosis: brain tumor.

I said to my surgeon: *We are supposed to go to Asia in three months. Is that still possible?* Marathon sinewy and I've-Seen-It-All pragmatic she said: *I don't see why not.* A week later, she cracked open my skull. I have a memory of the surgery: My spirit said, *I'm getting the hell out of here.* And my body—as though commanding a dog—yelled, *Stay!* Dave fed me and bathed me, gently shampooing around the stapled-and-glued gash. Spinal fluid gushed and clicked in my skull. Even he could hear the symphony of healing.

Three months later, we were greeted by a purple Hong Kong sky. Typhoon Haiyan's tail whipped the hotel's rooftop infinity pool. For the first time since the surgery, I submerged my head. Baptism. Rain pelted us at a slant, and the pool water rose and fell in waves. The wind was so strong it almost toppled us over as we moved from pool to Jacuzzi. Dave said, *We'll be okay as long as the building stands.* I thought about the surgeon busting into my skull. I thought about all those elevators and jets and boats and taxis and subways hoisting our bodies up and down and whizzing them through space and time. I thought about the faith it takes to live life in the face of complete and total impermanence. I said, *Even if the building fell, we'd be okay.* He smiled and nodded. It was an infinity pool, after all. We held out our arms like wings and yelled into the skyscraper skyline, into the howling winds: *To infinity and beyond!*

Sage Curtis

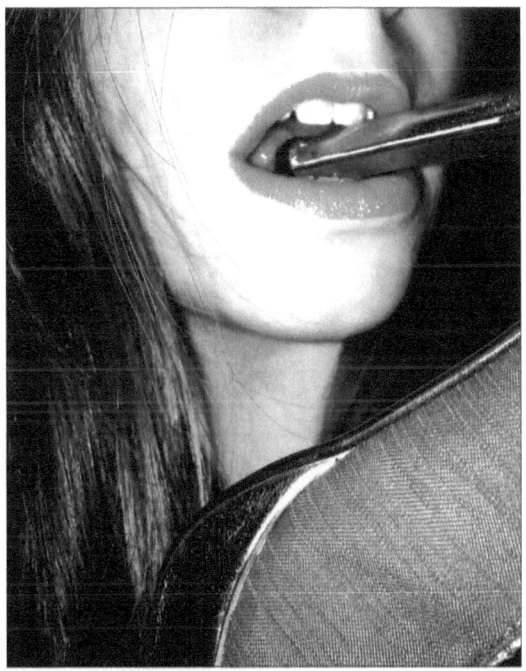

Neon night

Smoke in pulsing air
caught in the purple light here
like thick twilight clouds.

A zipper, the back
of my dress, your shirt buttons,
they all come undone.

My stiletto like
a cigarette in your mouth.
You should see me burn.

3

Mark Heinlein

After walks I see clearly

Mark Heinlein

Three

After walks I see clearly

Nahida S. Nisa

An outrageous declaration

Your author is a beautiful woman. Her hair swallows the stars and arranges them; she is small enough to be taken by the sea. She has hands too elegant for the feminine glove. Around her neck and in her hair, she wears constellations, trophies she has given herself, symbols of her liberation. (Here, your author pauses to wonder whether she thinks like a conqueror, cautiously.) Your author is a beautiful woman. She fears permanence, yet longs for eternity.

In your author's ancestry, the reddening of lips. In your author's ancestry, the most precious of scents. She remembers she is mostly water. Your author was raised on the sweetness of honey, on the kisses of drops of roses and jasmine. Her skin is lined with green, lit with the ethereality of gold. Your author measures salt; she knows the sea is preserved. She was born of the sea.

Your author is a beautiful woman. Her eyes are large and deep because the night stirs within her and gives rise to the moon. Her legs are long in the sand. Do not think of your author's tongue. It is too civilized to speak your language. A tender ring of music. Your author is a beautiful woman. This is a revolution.

Bob Woodward

Going south

In March 1960, my friend Guy and I decided to hitchhike to Florida over spring break. A classmate gave us a ride from our Connecticut college campus to New Jersey where we were deposited on the Jersey Turnpike to thumb in vain for hours and were about to call it quits when a large moving van pulled over. The driver told us we could sleep in the back on or in what he was hauling to Rockingham, North Carolina. And sleep we did, Guy on a couch and me in the backseat of a 1953 Buick Roadmaster four-door sedan.

It was mid-morning when the van's rear doors swung open and we walked out into a balmy spring day. We stuck out our thumbs and five hours later without any luck walked to the Rockingham Greyhound bus station, laid down $20 for tickets as far into Georgia as we could get. From there, we thought it would be easy to hitchhike to Atlanta and then on south. We sat in the front two seats of the bus. An hour into the trip, the bus stopped to pick up passengers. On trooped a group of college age, fit looking African-American men and women. They dutifully went to sit in the back of the bus and we soon followed to find out that they were a track team from an all-black college on their way to a dual meet. We talked track, we talked music (yes, Guy and I dug Ray Charles), and we talked about post-college plans.

When our stop came, we shook hands and hugged our new friends. As we walked to the roadside store/bus stop, a large man who got off the bus behind me jostled me with his shoulder and then pushed Guy with a forearm. Another disembarking passenger spit at us. "What are you Yankee boys doing sitting with the coloreds?" he barked. Once inside the store, we were denied service and told it would be best if we "weren't seen in this area again." We walked five miles out of town, slept in a cornfield that night and were able to hitch to Atlanta the next day and spend what money we had left on bus tickets north. We sat in the back of the bus.

Kate Reid

Finding sunny weather

W e're here, wherever we are." I'm staring at the first line of a journal entry. The blinds of the room are drawn providing only foggy slits of light and the navy of the walls builds the darkness. The awkward state of being in my 14-year-old mind, armed with the clarity of hindsight, makes me blush. The sentence isn't written with sarcasm. They are not the words of a youth paying careful attention to ambivalence. I didn't know where we were just as if you asked me what time it was I could possibly tell you, and if you asked me what month it was I could guess with a certain ingenuity, but if you asked me what day of the week it was I was certain to have no clue. The name of the place meant little to me and means little to me now. Islands in the South Pacific do that. An atoll is very similar to any other atoll. I match the date of my entry to a date in our logbook because I need to reference you and locate "here" as Apataki, an atoll amongst a series in French Polynesia called The Tuamotos. We arrive just shy of a six-day passage and the visibility is shit. It's been squalling on and off the whole approach. We hit the pass early in the afternoon and it's slack water perfectly, but grey overcast means we can't eyeball navigate around coral heads and it takes us two tries to get in. My mother and I act as human radars and man each side of the deck straining our eyes for potentials hazards while my father is at the helm. Broken clouds and spots of sun eventually break the grey. We manage the mile and a half pass successfully and lay anchor at the tiny atoll that is nothing but a bump of sand and palms in a pool of turquoise.

Despite our hopes, squally weather returns after only a few hours and deciding the left shore's no good, we'll have to leave for Tuao. Our anchor chain is wrapped up on a massive head of coral, and we bend one of the bow rollers trying to get up. "NO GOOD!" My father's shoulder-length white hair whips erratically in the wind. "STUCK!" I can just make him out through the beads of rain gathering on the dodger as he motions us to stop reversing on the chain. We could physically untangle the chain, but the weather makes it too unsafe to put a diver in the water. The biggest squall hits from the southeast around 3PM with 37-knot winds and 4 foot fetch waves. With daylight nearly gone we become effectively trapped as diving on the chain is not an option and abandoning it completely to leave the anchorage becomes a last resort. We are dog tired from the previous passage and our night is sleepless. But it's a northwest anchorage and the wind has turned southeast and now it's a lee shore. We're clocked stern to atoll and if our chain pops free of the coral, we'll blow onto the reef and be pummeled like a toy ship in a washing machine. There's no real option of departure. Navigating through the pass at night in this weather offers only a thin chance of escape, and a reef bordering the shore offers certain destruction. Every sound on a boat is magnified by the hull. What comes back to me about that night perhaps most clearly above all else except the fear was the grinding retch of the chain on coral, drumming into our skulls, comforting only in its ability to keep us awake.

We motor into the wind all night and hobbyhorse sickly in the fetch, fighting the pressure off the anchor chain. At a certain point late into the night I remember leaving the cockpit. "Kate, just go try and sleep," said my mother. I lay in the v-berth and cried instead because there was nowhere I could go and nothing else we could do and I was afraid to lose my home and I was afraid of the dark and the wet and the thrashing weather. People who aren't sailors fear the open ocean in the same way that most people fear flying in planes, the lack of anything concrete. But let me assure you that to a sailor, land is much more daunting than the inconstant vastness of the ocean. Boats are built for water and weather and these things don't punch holes in hulls. For the rest of the night I held a metal pin of an angel that my grandmother had given me. That night I held that pin till the edges of the wings dug into my hand and it hurt. The reaction seems silly to me now, an embarrassingly youthful dramatization. But my fear was real, and so I suppose was my response. I didn't know if I believed in God, hell, if I'm any closer to figuring that out now, but in that moment my grandmother's trust was good enough for me and I prayed. I guess that's what people do when they're stuck; they find a little faith. When the morning finally came, the squall died. My dad was able to dive on the anchor and untangle the chain from the coral. In a neon blue swim skin and red and black fins it occurred to me that he probably seemed just a giant kin to the tropical fish below. Soon after the wind turned. Something happens when the wind shifts in warm places, like a giant exhale and then—I stood at the bow and followed the chain with my eyes and the bright colors of the coral were strong and clear. The only disruption to the viscous surface of the water was the dancing reflection of the sun in a cloudless blue sky. The beach was a perfect scar of white swept clear by the wind and rain and the green fronds of the palms stretched unconcerned by the night's assault—it was paradise.

Rainsong

Moonlight in the dawn—
east mountain dusted in frost,
absence of birdsong.

What of this winter?
The unhappy song of rain,
your shape again changes.

Years turning from me,
quiet days ever numbered.
In us, the dust of stars.

Gayle Lubeck

Whiteout

S taying too long in Chichen Itza, Mexico while waiting for the young couple who were our partners on the aircraft to descend from the tallest pyramid, was an unforeseen error. I was weary by this point in our visit. Daniel had gotten plastered the evening before, drinking too many margaritas at the bar, and wanted to talk most of the night. We had risen at 6:00 a.m. to make the jaunt to the small airport to enter into the tiny Cessna. Our hotel was in Cozumel, a cab and a plane ride away. The flight was scheduled for 8:00 a.m. so that we would have time to revel in all of the ancient architectural wonders. In that part of the world, the weather has a tendency to interrupt flight plans, and it is best to leave Chichen Itza as early as possible. By the time the four of us reached the plane, at 1:30 p.m., the sky had already begun to formulate dark blustery storm clouds. I sensed some hesitancy on the part of the pilot, but ignored it. I was so worn out that all I wanted to do was board, rest, land, and go back to the hotel in one piece.

Daniel and I were seated in the back and our flight mates were seated facing us. As we lifted off, the white clouds began to envelop the entire plane, leaving zero visibility for the pilot.

I had heard of this type of air debacle before, but had never personally experienced it. I closed my eyes, said a short prayer to God asking for safe passage and began to doze off into my own state of oblivion. Just prior to fully engaging in slumber, I heard the sounds of the other passengers. They were moaning. The woman was beginning to cry. I thought to myself, what babies, and gladly curled up closer to Daniel.

I felt the aircraft tumbling through the atmosphere and briefly opened my eyes to spy on the aviator who was calm. I had been through much worse turbulence than this, I thought, and just slept. After about half an hour, I awakened to see the most enchanting rainbow. It was right next to the craft. I noticed both the beginning and the end of it, springing up from the jungle floor below. Its vibrant colors were a symbol of victory. We indeed had gotten through the white-out unscathed. Perhaps it was my initial prayer to the Great Beyond that was a catalyst in our secure return. I will never know for sure, but looking back on that adventure now, I think that something mystical was at work on our behalf.

Christopher Danaher

Second helping

What do Kibbeh and a job interview have in common? Well, one is a ground meat dish, often served raw, garnished with pine nuts and olive oil; the other can sometimes seem like a meat grinder—or a pleasant meal, depending on the outcome. And, sometimes, depending on whether the interviewer has had his morning coffee.

When my grandfather was alive, he preferred Sanka crystals. In the 1970s, when my grandfather was a successful businessman, freeze-dried instant coffee was a space-age invention that helped people wake up and be their best: Sanka and enthusiasm. Instant coffee was part of my grandfather's Easter ritual which also included gathering his extended family (six children, their spouses, many grandchildren, and countless family friends who were all "uncle" or "aunt") for a family feast. This tradition usually included a large dish of ground meat in the center of the table, and one particularly shy grandson practicing his public speaking for the crowd. "Hi, my name is Chris," he would stutter, thinking that it was the Gettysburg Address. The crowd would chew and nod politely, whispering about other things. The child thought that they were hanging on his every word; he felt pressure to say something good. In hindsight, they were probably thinking, "Yes, we know. We were part of the conversation about what to name the baby."

Today I have a job interview that could change my life. I am nervous, and hopeful. In the shower this morning, getting ready to head into the grinder, I find myself thinking about that dish of raw meat; about the crowd of whispering faces that surrounded it, ready to tear it apart; and about that enthusiastic old man who was smiling because his family was together—and because he had patient confidence, and complete faith, that his awkward grandson would *be somebody* someday (pass the Sanka, please).

Pranita Patel

Nature's trimmings

Tom Leikam

The dance - in three movements

I
The cold of winter recedes
a cherry blossom beckons
spring's woodwinds drive darkness away

II
a cacophony of radiant sound
a pearl of rain falls
in prayer the world form

III
life is awakening
to the unfolding dance
the symphony begins

Jesse Mardian

10 seconds

Ocean Beach Sunday Morning: I don't ride the big ones often, and I don't let on that I am terrified. What a coward I am—with these boys who've surfed Puerto and Pipe, these men who are not afraid to drop in late and be swallowed. We flip on our hoods, grab our boards, and paddle out. The fear is bowel-deep, my lips cracked, my mouth dry. I think of the warm San Clemente summers, the head-high happy waves I grew up in. The surging current moves north towards the Golden Gate. There is a small rip and I follow it out unscathed, the mist curling off of towering sets down the beach.

Wait for the right one—the wave of least resistance—and everything will be just fine. Blairsy goes, and so does Dr. Jones, down these thick, tubing monsters that roar when they detonate. The offshore breeze freezes my bones as I sit outside the break, nothing but a buoy. Soon I know I must take a wave, so I find a safe, unthreatening shoulder and take off. *This is not so bad; I can do this for an hour.* How spineless. But as I paddle back out, I see the sets forming and I know I am not going to make it.

The mountain of a wave collapses before me, transforming into an avalanche of whitewash. Just ditch the board and swim under; there's nothing to it. I dip below the surface, penciling down into the icy Pacific. Not deep enough. And as the wave grabs me in its fist and throws me into a maelstrom of violent twirls, I try to remain calm. I let my body go limp as I was taught. *Just let yourself go along for the ride.* But I am beaten down deeper, and as soon as the air in my lungs thins, I panic. No floor to push from, no surface in sight, and still I flip in this perpetual washing machine. Searching for my leash, my lifeline, my umbilical chord, the wave tugs at my limbs. I find the leash and climb it! An abyss of the darkest green fills my vision as I open my eyes. The leash brushes past my fingers, but I can't get a hold. The unrelenting force weighs upon me. Seconds seem so much longer when you panic. *This is it. I'm going to drown. I'm going to drown. Drown.* And as the last air in my lungs trickles away like the sand in an hourglass, the wave lets go. It dies. I am free to swim and the dark water lightens. I finally shatter through the surface, breathe for the first time in twenty-six years.

The teacher

Should dark clouds persist?
Should the chill and warmth compete?
Nature contemplates.

Eternal sunshine
Is our hope from day to day.
Beings contemplate.

A blend helps us grow.
The epiphany arrives.
Nature teaches well.

Jeri McCutcheon

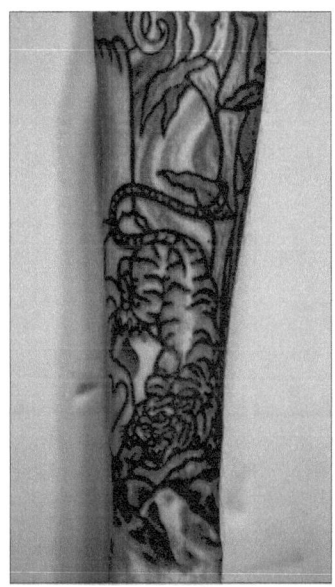

Arm tiger

shades of orange and black
camouflage in the tall grass
golden eyes stare

darkness brings about
patiently crouching, silent
courageous tiger

quiet still waters
reflecting discernment
long winding path

Belinda Hopkinson

Higher ground

W hen I boarded the New York City subway that afternoon of August 14th, 2003, I could never have imagined what would transpire. I had travelled from England, spent a few lovely days with a friend in Brooklyn, and was now daydreaming about my two-week movement training west of the city. Suddenly, the subway car came to a halt. The lights dimmed, and the air conditioning stopped. It was the height of summer, nearly 90 degrees, and 80 percent humidity. Small emergency lights came on. Silence. Then, a brief intercom announcement stating there was a city-wide electricity outage. My heart began to race uncontrollably. Could this be another attack? I looked around me at the array of reactions. There was a young couple in love, smiling and relaxed; a mother looking anxious, pulled her two young children close; a middle-aged man began to talk increasingly louder, referring to the 1977 city-wide blackout when there had been looting in the streets. I tried to calm my thumping heart, but to no avail. Then, to my dismay, the train driver came through, locking all interconnecting doors. My fear ramped up a notch. I heard myself say aloud, "I'm scared." A woman my age answered,

"You'll see, it'll be fine." An hour and a half went by slowly, so slowly. She then confided that she was desperate to go to the bathroom. I offered to set up a place in the corner for her, walled off by my suitcase, and that we could sing and whistle together while she pee'd into a plastic bag. After some laughter, she agreed and was liberated. Helping her got me out of myself, but I still had a racing heart. Then, I noticed a man had jimmied the lock of an interconnecting door and was preparing to get off the train. I peered through the dark window, and, yes—a miracle—we had actually drawn into a station but were on the far side of the tracks. I heard myself say "I'm getting off," and like an arrow, headed with my gear to the door. I had a flashlight with me and lit the man's climb down to the tracks. In less than a few minutes, he was across the tracks, up on the platform, gone, and back again to tell me that the exit was just a few hundred feet away! A rush of relief came over me. I then heaved my suitcase down the steep metal steps, gingerly crossed the third rail, and the man helped me pull myself up onto the platform. The woman on the train followed me, but no one else did.

Out of the near darkness and the self-made prison of fear, I was very soon free in a bright, sunlit Manhattan street, teeming with people walking in all directions. The sun felt reassuring, and I made a few phone calls from a public pay phone, the only telephone circuitry that seemed to be functioning. A good friend at my final destination advised, "Make sure by sundown to have decided where you are going to sleep." The place that instantly came to mind as a safe haven: a church. I asked a passer-by where the nearest church was, and it turned out Grace Church was just a stone's throw away. I pulled my suitcase the few blocks, walked through the small black iron garden gate into the quiet churchyard, and sat down on the grass. Respite, at last. I noticed that three young men were looking rather intently at me. I looked back at them, then turned my gaze away to notice a large sign stating that Grace Church would be closed for the summer for renovations. Sigh. One of the three young men then asked me if I was OK. My self-protection antennae were up, but I trusted my intuition. A conversation ensued; they explained they were colleagues from a film company considering making a short movie about people who went to churchyards during a crisis. I wasn't sure whether to believe that, but explained I was looking for a church to sleep in for the night. We exchanged first names, and C. told me he could walk me to another church nearby where his baby daughter was recently baptized. My trust was growing. We set off as a group of four, walking through the crowded streets, but it turned out that other church was closed for renovations, too! C. told me it would be unlikely he would be able to drive back to his family that evening because of heavy, blocked traffic. He said that he had been a child during the 1977 outage and how aspects of that experience had frightened him. He assured me he would stay with me until I reached my next destination. An angel in disguise? I asked where his office was and whether there was access to the roof. I wanted to sleep on a roof where I imagined there would be greater safety from any people in buildings leaving candles unattended. I knew all NYC buildings have external fire escapes, and I could clamber down one of those, if needed. C. told me that their office was on the 12th and last floor of a building, with direct access to the roof—another miracle! We set off together, eating some of my camping fruit and nut bars. Along the way, we saw that groceries and restaurants had closed their doors and lowered their metal security curtains. Our hunger and thirst were growing.

Little could we ever have foreseen that in the darkened office building, as we made our way up the eleven flights of stairs, a door would open as we reached the fourth floor, a warm voice welcoming us in to take a rest. It was a theatre company that had had to cancel their show for the evening, but they had fresh fruit as props, and cookies and bottled water for intermission. I could hardly believe our luck! After making a phone call (from their phone line with a jack) to family to reassure them and also indicate the address where I would be sleeping, we left and made our way up the stairwell. Two of the guys settled into the office, lighting candles for the night. C. and I climbed out to the roof. Suddenly, there we were in the heights, under the full moon, the Manhattan skyline in unlit silhouette. With a view onto the Empire State Building, there were no city sounds except for a few police and news helicopters overhead. The quiet urban beauty was striking. The day had been unexpected and surreal. What was real was the solid presence of strangers who had appeared as though by grace to provide help, companionship, and shelter. Unable to sleep, C. and I talked through the night, save a couple of hours dozing off before dawn. He told me about his life, how it had unfolded so far, and all the reasons that he considered himself the luckiest man in the world. He asked me about my life. Later in the morning, driving through empty streets with no traffic lights, he dropped me off at my good friend's in Brooklyn, just around the corner from where he was dropping off his colleague. C. had indeed been a guardian angel in the form of a stranger. Now, more than ten years later, I realize again how lucky I have been, and am reminded how the journey from darkness to light, from the depths to the heights, can often be a matter of synchronicity, trust, and unfolding connections.

Sarju Naran

Memory foam mattress

Damn, memory foam
It remembers me heavy
But now I've lost weight

It once was my nest
But now has lost all support
Now a sunken pit

Climb into my mold
Its memory doesn't fade
Like a dense steel trap

Green light go

I pull up to a red light. The lanes to my right and to my left are both empty. I'm driving my recently purchased Mini Cooper. It's a lot sportier than I am. It makes me feel young and I sing along with the radio. I'm distracted and resist the urge to check my phone. I really need to pay attention because I'm in the process of reacquainting myself with the art of driving a manual transmission. Since I haven't driven one in fifteen years, I sometimes forget about the clutch. Another car pulls up directly behind me. Did I mention the traffic light was at the top of a small hill?

The light turns green. I forget about the clutch. The car stalls. I make eye contact in my rearview mirror with the guy behind me. He's waving his hands to encourage me to move and I mouth the word "sorry!" He lays on the horn, loud and angry, which makes me nervous and my car stalls again. This time I mouth a word to him that is not "sorry!" but considerably meaner. It might have been "asshole" or "go around me, idiot." Or worse. He blasts the horn in anger. I might have used my middle finger to indicate my annoyance. My car stutters then successfully shifts into first. When we arrive at the next red light, my nemesis pulls up beside me in the left lane and rolls down his passenger side window. I roll down my window to say "Sorry, I stalled," but he doesn't hear me as he shouts, "You don't have to be such a fucking bitch!" I scream, "I am not a bitch! You're an asshole! What are you going to do, get out of your car and punch me in front of all these witnesses? Go ahead, jackass!" The upper half of my body is sticking out the car window as I say this. My steely hair is whipping in the wind; it is electrified and exploding around my head. The drivers in the cars around us are looking on nervously.

The light changes. I shift the car into first, roll up my window and drive home with the blood still pounding in my ears. I rage for hours thinking of all the things I should have said. I struggle with the murderous thoughts ricochetting around in my brain. Finally, I breathe. I think about how this man who was so angry is not much different than I am. In a flash we both went crazy, violent. I work at it the rest of the day and eventually it comes to me. I need to shift gears. I say to myself, "He's probably carrying a heavy burden. Maybe his mother died recently or his cousin attempted suicide. Maybe he is worried about a sick child or doesn't have a job." I practice compassion. I let it go.

Ashley Florimonte

Tenacity

Audacity
Enveloped in silence,
a primal yawn
awakes.

Chamomile
Hands on the wall
lay silent
beneath the drapes.

Watches
Among the shadows,
a curious sun
will exhale

Privileged

Befor you get off the plane, even before you reach the door, hot and humid air bursts forth to smother you with its welcoming hugs and kisses—like an overbearing relative faking their best enthusiasm at seeing you again. Welcome travelers, if you can't stand the heat then get the hell out of India. Guards in berets, dark sunglasses, and armed with rifles are the next to greet us—a site made odder because of the cheerful and pleasant natives further behind them and the dark night sky even further beyond. This place with no air conditioning, this place where guards where sunglasses at night, this place with signs warning us of taxi scams—no, this place made no sense to us at all. What made the least sense it seemed was why, as all 72 of us were stalled by our taxi drivers hassling us to be paid before they drove out of the airport parking lot, a scraggly thin boy who looked to be about ten was pinned down by two of the guards. Or how that boy kept angrily yelling and glaring at the passing cars and taxis. Or how, after he was shooed off by the guards after they gave him one more warning, the boy threw another rock at a passing taxi and ran off before the guards got a hold of him again. No, that made no sense; we were Americans, we were on a pilgrimage, and we had money to prove both—why wouldn't the kid want us in his country?

The cold is prevalent as the sun hasn't even risen, yet a mass of over a hundred people push and shove to get through the gates. It's a scene straight from a Black Friday shopping experience—that is, if it weren't for the little kids trying to sell us bouquets of lotus flowers, the glaring guards armed with batons shouting for us to form a single line, and the aggressive pushy Buddhist devotees. No, this would be Black Friday for Buddhists, India style. The monks—some beggars in disguise— and devotees push and shove and wouldn't hesitate to trample over someone all for a spot closest to the Bodhgaya tree where Buddha obtained enlightenment or for the front seats to, yet another, golden Buddha statue. For those beggars in disguise, it's all about those prime donation spots—earning thousands of rupees a day for "meditating" and all you have to do is wake up before dawn, sounds like a great deal. For the devotees, it's ensuring that our Masters have the prime spot to meditate and chant—to show that our group is more spiritually pure than everyone else we beat there. After all, who cares about practicing the faith—it's all about how close you are to the sacred places and how much money you stuff in the donation box that adds up to spiritual enlightenment, right? If the bits of rupees that stick out of the overstuffed donation boxes are any indication, it seems everyone here agrees. At the very least, it'll add up to an impressive picture you can post on Facebook and brag to all your friends back home in the States—which is all that really matters.

It isn't difficult to show "devotion" and "charity" when you get sixty rupees to the dollar and the native merchants and beggars know it. It's practically un-American *not* to throw some money at a problem before us; but in one of the poorest sections in India, as the little children carrying their younger siblings follow along gesturing for money, we walk away and we must because it's our lives on the line. Worse than being trampled for a prime worshipping spot, those dusty, ragtag, pitiful kids wouldn't hesitate to cling onto your pale foreign body and drag you down to the dusty ground because the rupees you hold is their life—it's an eye for an eye and a life for a life. What good is the money we wave around so proudly as Americans when it cannot help those that need it the most—when we must fear for our own lives because those most pitiful are also the most dangerous. We've stuffed our money in donation boxes that are almost at their bursting point, we've made sure that every monk's donation bowl is never empty after our group passes by, and some even angered our Master by putting rupees into the hands of teachers—red-faced from humiliation. Money solves everything—are we really to abandon that American ideology here? But thanks to American ingenuity, we always find a loophole—here Mr. Assistant Bus driver, *you* give them that money for us.

Brian Foss

Absolute Calvin in Los Banos

Calvin's evil scheme
make inner wear outer wear
a Calvinist rails

new liquor store rules
right driver's license data
and right decorum

Calvin rolls to bank
amazed his pants so inspire
John Calvin rolls over

Kristen Austin

The boy in the dark

I saw his face for only a second, wide-eyed, terror-stricken, desperate. How could a dark-skinned face look so white? The boy was ghostly, really, standing on the side of the road with a broken bicycle, wearing that black-and-white striped shirt. I caught only a glimpse of him in the headlights of our car. And when I turned to look out the back window, he had already dissolved into the inky-black darkness. That sweltering night, decades ago now, was as dark and thick as black-bean soup.

"Did you guys see that?" I asked over the thudding pulse in my ears. No one in our vehicle so much as flinched. The silence was deafening, nothing but the droning hum of tires on pavement and the unspoken words that surrounded an urgent need to put this place behind us as fast as possible. "Aren't you going to stop?" Our car sped down the two-lane highway. It cut through a dense, impenetrable jungle like a part on the scalp of Mexico.

"Oldest trick in the book." Louis, my then brother-in-law, said, vestiges of a Mexican accent re-emerging. He punched the gas pedal with his foot, picking up speed. "What do you mean?

He's just a boy!" I had grown frantic, fingering the diamond on my new wedding ring. My then-husband nodded in agreement, so quiet, so stoic. "Banditos. He's a decoy. You stop and dozens of them come out of the jungle and jump you, take everything you got, including your car. Then it's you on the side of the road, if you are still alive." Louis' tone was so matter of fact. "You sure?" I felt stupid, yet still overwhelmed with guilt. How could we ever know unless we tried?

Melissa Becker

Evening

Orange streaks and pink hues
Dance along the horizon—
The sun gives goodnight.

Leaves like season wings—
The cold plucks them from the branch
To admire city lights.

A chorus sounds,
Thousands of violins sing—
Crickets lull nature.

Obscurity

Unbeknownst to us
We are hidden only by our
Feigned obscurity

And that steel barbed wire
We so carefully tried to
Wrap around our hearts

Will tear deeper wounds
When we decide to rip it off
And be found at last

Tara Phillips

Autopsy

You've never even seen a dead body before. You roll the rickety x-ray machine over a metal-strip threshold, and the floor changes from fresh glossed, waxy white to a neglected, dull gray. The sterile scent of disinfectant lingers here in the older part of the building, but it's mixed with a dank smell of something like dust. Something aged, dark. Following signs that lead you to the morgue and the autopsy rooms, you stop outside the one marked "Autopsy Room 2." You press a tiny button and wait. A woman opens the door and hands you a pair of powder blue, disposable shoe covers, a matching surgical hat like a flimsy shower cap, and a pale yellow paper mask to wear over your mouth and nose. You put the items on; the woman hands over a container of alcohol wipes and tells you to wipe down the x-ray machine. You walk in behind her then, pushing the machine in front of you. You wonder what her job title is, but you don't ask. She whistles as she leads the way, and as you enter, she introduces you as "The New X-ray Gal." At once, there's an unforgettable stench you assume is formaldehyde. It's mixed with the sterile odor of alcohol and something else. Something sour. The sharpness of it, even through the mask, is enough to make your eyes water as if you've cut onions. Three or four women stand at various stations with sinks and metal counter tops, working with small plastic bags and labels, wearing hats and masks like the ones you're wearing. A towering black man with a week's worth of stubble on his face sings along to a tune on the radio, something from the eighties, bobs his head. He stops singing just long enough to greet you. The man wears a long white, fluid-resistant gown, blue hat, and yellow mask like the rest of you, and he stands over a silver examination table, holding a large empty plastic bag. You wonder what his job title is, but you don't ask. *Hi*, you say.

You look down at the table. What you see, you won't forget; on the table, a young girl, you'd guess nine or ten years old, but you'd be wrong. She lies still on the cold sterling table, naked. Pallid skin, limbs stiffened. Her hair is matted and brittle, her mouth slightly opened, her eyes closed. A blue paper sheet rests over her pelvis, and you think about how uncomfortable she would be if she were aware. If she could feel the chill of the table beneath her, the hardness of it. If she could smell the rankness of the air in the room. If she were aware that she is naked in a room with this man, the others, and you. If she were alive, you wonder, would she cry out for her mother or father, struggle to get off the table and out of the room? You wish she could. The tall man tells you the stats: African American female, age seven. Found by uncle in her home. No apparent abrasions or other obvious injuries. Respiratory failure, cause unknown. He speaks of the date and time she was found, and the approximate time of death. The home she was found in was filthy and poor. There were indications of neglect. You are asked to do several x-rays as part of an investigative autopsy on the suspicion of child abuse. The x-rays will indicate whether there was unusual trauma to any part of the girl's body. The man holds out his hand and asks you to give him the first x-ray cassette. "We'll start with a skull: AP view," he says. You hand him the proper size cassette and he slips it into the plastic bag, places it under the child's head. You position your x-ray machine over her face and adjust the collimator and exposure factors, stand back, and make the first exposure. He removes the x-ray cassette and hands it back to you. You label it and set it aside. "Next view, skull: lateral view." You hand him another cassette. You repeat this process fourteen or fifteen times, different views of various body parts, from head to toe. The man continues to sing along with the radio between exchanges of the x-ray cassettes.

When you're finished, the tall man and the women at their stations thank you. You thank them too, for their help, and you give the man a nod as you back your machine out into the corridor. One of the women helps you with the door. You wipe down your machine again, wash your hands, and head back toward the Radiology department. The halls are quiet. The silence feels appropriate. Necessary. You think about the girl. She's someone's daughter, someone's granddaughter. Somebody's playmate at school on a swing set or singing rhymes while jumping rope. You wonder how many more times in your career you'll be expected to test your tolerance of things. Whether it'll harden you. Whether someday you'll sing along and bob your head to a song on the radio as a seven year-old child lies motionless on a stainless steel table.

Christopher Danaher

Something borrowed something blue

I have gained a lot from the unforgiving rocks of the Adirondack Mountains. As a sport climber, protected by strong ropes and specialized gear, I have gained a temporary reprieve from the paralyzing fear of heights that plagued me as a child, complicating family trips to the Empire State Building and even to the second floor of the National Air & Space Museum with its all-glass railings. I have gained new friendships with the staff at Adirondack Rock & River guide service who have trudged through the woods, who made sure that the ropes which held us as we climbed were tied correctly, and who pointed out which routes to avoid when the nesting falcons became aggressive in springtime. I have gained a renewed closeness with the members of my family for whom a trip to Keene Valley has become a yearly tradition, to visit places with names like Barkeater Cliff, and The Beer Walls. I gained a wife when I proposed to my sweetheart on a cliff edge of Owl's Head Mountain, down on one knee, wearing a heavy backpack and a grin as wide as the sunset. But this is not that kind of story.

This story is about something that I lost: a shoe. Not an ordinary shoe, but an ergonomically fitted approach shoe, the kind used for hiking to and from a rock face that you want to climb. In fact, I was wearing that very shoe when I proposed to my wife. I was wearing it as we hiked through the forest in eager anticipation of sharing a climb up Chapel Pond Slab. At the base of The Slab, we put on special climbing shoes to ascend the rock face. Our plan was to climb up The Slab and enjoy a bird's eye view of Chapel Pond and Keene Valley below before hiking back down. We carried our hiking shoes with us by clipping them to the back of our climbing harnesses for the long walk down from the top of the mountain. The climb was quick and fun, until we reached the top. That is where we lost it. My soon-to-be wife lost some skin from her knee, pushing herself through the crux of the climb with great determination, leaving behind a small red stain. Unbeknownst to me at the time, that is also where I lost one of the hiking shoes that had been clipped to my harness. We looked all over, but could not find my shoe on The Slab, nor back at the base of the climb. It was a long walk back wearing the thinly-soled climbing shoes, feeling every pebble and stick in the mud along the way. My shoe was gone. That was the end of it; until the next year when my wife and nephew and I were driving our rental car near Chapel Pond, and I saw something that caused me to stomp on the brakes. There was my shoe, atop a fence post by the side of the road. We all got out of the car to admire it. We had fun taking pictures of ourselves with my old shoe, along with the little white spiders who had made it their home during the many months that the shoe had been exposed to the elements. We smiled and posed, celebrating like we had found a treasure. Later someone would tell us that the shoe had spent the past year serving as a landmark, sometimes at the base of Chapel Pond Slab, marking the start of the climb, and sometimes out near the road, marking the trailhead of the hike to The Slab. We felt reunited with a long-lost, if much smellier and spider-infested, friend. We felt part of the folklore of one of our favorite places. We had lost a shoe, but had gained a day of smiles, and a lifetime of memories.

I have lost a lot to the unforgiving rocks of the Adirondack Mountains. I have lost some knuckle skin and a few drops of blood, jamming my hands into cracks in the rocks while climbing. I have lost some climbing gear, favorite carabiners dropped from nervous hands at high altitudes. I have lost the shoe that I was wearing when I proposed to my wife. Sometimes, thinking about those things makes me sad. But this is not that kind of story.

Sarah Lyn Rogers

Grey

Through the glass pane: sky,
muted as my impulses.
And yet expansive.

My blood is not mine.
For whom does it run? (Not me.)
In my soul, a drought.

Clouds are forming, filled
with brilliant hues. Remember?
I will call the rain.

Tom Leikam

On the line

I have just come up from the creek. Mom is sitting at the kitchen table sipping her coffee when she asks me where've I been. "Down the creek watching the quail." Then, out of the blue, she looks at me and says, "You know, killing and violence are stupid." My gut is filled with butterflies, my skin tingles—in that instant I know the sacredness of all life and that I could never profane that sacredness. It would be like taking a gun, pointing it at my head and pulling the trigger. In fact, I knew that that would be precisely what I would do. In the years to come, this conviction would be tested. After the poisoning and death of my favorite dog, Stuffy, a seminal moment lashed out at me like a bullwhip. I had the chance to avenge Stuffy's death. My brothers had a confession from the kids who lived in the orchard. I was to fight the youngest since I was the youngest in my family. We gathered in the orchard. My opponent stepped toward me—fists clenched. I looked directly into his eyes. I then turned to my brothers and, looking at them, turned my back and walked away disgusted. Violence would have solved nothing. In the years to come I would be challenged to the depths of my soul.

Months pass after my last Academic Deferment ran out before I received my Induction Papers. On the drive to the Induction Center my mind travels back to my encounter where, in the crucible of an interrogation room, a group of six men tried to shake me to the core of my beliefs. It was a fifteen-round slug fest. My soul, my beliefs, were planted squarely in the center of the room—I wasn't going to get knocked out. Not ever! In the end the six were deadlocked. But, there had been a seventh member who didn't attend the interrogation and who without ever meeting me voted "Nay!" Everything had been a sham. My anger at this almost ripped me apart. Once at the Induction Center all of us who have reported are placed in a room and lined up against the walls. We are told to strip to our skivvies. The physical exam begins. After blood pressure I go to the hearing test. As I exit the hearing test I am told: "Your hearing will be worse when you get back from Nam." Then off to the psychologist who asks me about filing for Conscientious Objector status. I say nothing and exit. It's all a farce—the military just wants bodies. My soul screams. There is a stigma associated with being a CO—we are no better than scum—to be kicked in the huevos unmercifully. Once the physicals are completed, we return to the original room and get dressed. We are then led to a curtained-off room where we are to take the Oath of Service. The room is intimidating—plush, deep red carpet, the American flag backdropped against the Great Seal of the United States. An Army Colonel stands on a raised dais looking down on us. Everyone is asked to take the Oath of Service and then to take a step forward. I do not take the oath, nor do I step forward. Once the oath is over I am asked to stay behind. Two Military Police now take me to a dark, dingy, poorly lit hallway. As the MPs leave, they snicker: "Remember, you can change your mind and avoid going to prison." I am left in solitude for hours. Eventually, I am sent up a creaky old staircase to see a WWII vet. He asks me where I am from; if I know what I am doing? He tries to sound fatherly. I exit. The two MPs take me back to the hallway and leave me in solitude for hours before returning and escorting me across the street to the Federal Jail. We enter through the back entrance where I have to pass inmates in holding cells. "Nice ass... Ooh, what fun with you." I have been told that within days of my incarceration I will be raped or gang banged. My mugshot is taken, I am fingerprinted, booked and let go on my own recognizance.

I have been waiting for this morning. The air is crisp as I enter the Post Office to pick up the Registered Letter. I open it. It reads: The United States of America vs. Thomas Alvin Leikam. As I read on I was instructed to report to the Federal Court in San José, where I would be given a public defender— Gary Patton Sr., one of the finest draft lawyers in the nation. We prepare to do grievous battle. My case is moved to San Francisco and I am handed over to Gary's son—Gary, Jr. I was expected to take the stand for about three hours of examination and cross- examination. Another slug fest. I was prepared in the course of the trial to have not only myself unmercifully attacked, but my family as well. No holds barred. Once in court, events take on a new dimension. When Judge Weigel enters, we are asked to stand. He takes the bench and we are told to sit down. Judge Weigel turns to the prosecutor and asks, "On what grounds is the defendant being tried?" "Failure to apply in a timely manner," is the response. Judge Weigel looks incredulously at the prosecutor: "Don't you have better grounds than that?" The Prosecutor is flabbergasted. He has no response. Judge Weigel turns and asks me to stand. Now I am nervous. I am not even asked to swear on the Bible. Judge Weigel begins: "Were you raised this way?" "Yes." "Are your parents in the room?" "Yes." He asks my parents to stand. "Did you raise your son this way?" In unison they reply, "Yes, sir." Then in one incredible bang of the gavel Judge Stanley Weigel declares, in a voice that reverberates through my soul and court house, "Case dismissed!" There is a sense of euphoria and as I walk down the Court House steps to the flow of life in the streets below, I know that delving into my core self, my principles of life clearly expressed themselves—so clearly there could have been no other outcome to this trial.

Brownlee Reed

Untitled

The Red Moon rises;
just above the copse, sinks a
kettle of vultures.

Lone bird spiders flock
together, migrating. Dens
nestle in creek beds.

Passing clouds shroud, then
reveal the earth below; star-
light reflects off stone.

The 91

I t's been over half an hour and we haven't moved more than twenty feet. A drop of sweat starts to inch down the back of my neck before racing down the length of my spine. I decide to wipe my forehead on the sky blue polo shirt that is my school uniform, peeling my arm off the armrest with an audible smack. The radio is on, but my Spanish is abysmal and I'm not paying attention so I have no clue what the two hosts are yattering on about. A song comes on that I actually know and understand the lyrics to, and Mom starts to belt it out as the traffic starts to let up. I smile, or at least try to. It was my fault we were 'late' in getting on the freeway. You wouldn't think it, but there's about an hour difference between 2:30PM and 3:00PM. My Mom keeps belting. "Que tontos, que locos, somos tu y yo!". I think about how sad the song is, despite being so damn catchy. It's about a couple that's in love, but both of them have "moved on" to other relationships even though they still think about each other all the time. At least, I think that's what it's about. I understand the songs better since I spent the summer in my Mom's hometown. I remember walking to the nearest shop for a soda within twenty minutes of arriving at my grandma's house, trudging up the uneven, stone- paved, road in the kind of weather that would make a patron of Hell complain. The shopkeeper took one look at me and yelled at her sister that my Mom was back in town.

I look at my Mom singing her head off, and briefly wonder if she sees herself in me, before pulling a book out of my bag. I know it won't last me the entire commute home, no book ever does, but I figure I might as well read it now that we still get the radio and Mom has something to entertain herself. I can keep her company when the radio dies....

The radio is dead. I listen as Mom talks to me about how much she misses my great- grandpa, a six foot three Yaqui Indian with mahogany skin and the bluest eyes you've ever seen. ...The radio is dead. I listen as Mom tells me about the piñata my grandpa made for her. Back when piñatas were made out of clay and throwing a party meant inviting the whole neighborhood... The radio is dead. I listen as Mom tells me how much she hated washing dishes as a teen. How she would trade my aunts all of their chores to avoid her turn to wash dishes, and how her first job in the states was as a dishwasher...The radio is dead. I listen as Mom tells me how happy she is that I got another Student of the Month Award. She reminds me of how well all my siblings did in elementary school...The radio is dead. I listen as Mom tells me about my Tio Chino, who isn't really my uncle but a close family friend, and how he used to be a bit of a cholo when he was younger. His then girlfriend and current wife used to carry a switchblade in her hair in case he got into trouble…The radio is dead. I listen as Mom tells me about how she disobeyed my grandpa's wishes when she came to the states on a student visa that she got with the help of my Nina Carmen…The radio is dead. I listen as Mom tells me about the porcelain tea set that was the reason she met Dad. At the time they met, he told her he had always thought that particular set would be for his wife. I wonder if I'll ever be that smooth…The radio is dead. I listen as Mom tries to act like everything is normal. I don't tell her I already know about the cysts they found…The radio is dead. Mom listens as I lie about why I'm struggling with middle school. …The radio is dead. I listen to another lecture about the importance of my studies;, I take notice of how often she brings up the idea of her not being around…The radio is dead. Mom wakes me up and tells me I was making sobbing noises. My sleeping pattern has become irregular. I tell her I can't remember what I was dreaming about. Years later I will wonder if this was when my insomnia started…The radio is dead. I listen as Mom tells me about the cysts they found. I start to worry it's bad news but then she tells me the radiation therapy worked. I act surprised that any of it happened…The radio is dead. I listen as Mom tells me about how proud she is that I'm graduating junior high. I apologize for not telling her

I was chosen to give the Graduate's Farewell. I wanted it to be a surprise. "It's ok," she says, and laughs. I recognize my own laughter in hers.

Candice Wynne

Ascension

Steadily
lifting one foot and then
the other
I rise to
find the height of
my potential

Three

PISMO BEACH, CALIFORNIA

Huayna Picchu, Peru

Three

Belinda Hopkinson

Awakening

The morning is cold
Sleeping bag—a warm cocoon
No wish to rise yet.

Light frame 'round the door
A bright shard through the curtain
The Sun's early call.

When sorrow visits
Fleeting beauty awakens
Solace in the soul

Alex Marroquin

The crow at the funeral

On a bright October day in New Orleans, three pigeons flutter by and land on the tree branch overlooking the Treme Community Center. Beside the building, a large sign drawn by local volunteers reads "Memorial Service of Herman Wallace," welcoming an oncoming group of mourners as they walk on dead yellow leaves on the sidewalk. Scott Crow towers over the other mourners. A small gust of wind blows through his grey hair as he stops in his path to let them inside of the community center before him. He comes across a few of Herman's relatives by the door and they thank him for attending the funeral service. With a somber voice, Scott replies that he wouldn't have missed it for the world. A single tear drips from his blue eyes as he grips the hands of Herman's niece. Scott tightly hugs Herman's other relatives before taking a seat at the front row. The community center is packed. Friends, family members, and supporting activists sit on the plastic chairs that face towards Herman's casket. Scott sits in the very front row where his family reserved a seat for him. As the crowd settles, the doors burst open as Robert King, a member of the Angola Three activist group, enters the room with other former members of the Black Panther Party. Robert straightens his tie and stands in the very front of the room. He humbly greets and thanks the guests. After clearing his throat, Robert begins to speak his tribute for his fallen comrade.

His voice proud, passionate, sweat dripping from his forehead, he talks about Herman's actions as a member of the Angola Three while imprisoned: spreading awareness of institutional racism and encouraging young, incarcerated black youths to renounce their criminal ways to fight for social justice. As Robert finishes, he pulls out a damp white rag from his shirt pocket and wipes the sweat off his face. He takes a deep breath before concluding his tribute with a prayer. Everyone in the room, including Scott, says Amen and Robert sits down with the guests. Everyone then stands and waits in line to pay their tribute to Herman Wallace. As the line moves along, Scott can't help feeling happiness for Herman. He feels relieved that Herman was able to spend his last two days on earth free from imprisonment, able to take his final breaths as a free man. When Scott takes his place at the front of the line, he looks down and sees Herman in the casket wearing his favorite collared shirt with matching jeans. His hands are folded neatly on his upper chest. Scott reaches into his pocket and retrieves Herman's trademark reading glasses. Memories of their relief efforts in the ruins of Hurricane Katrina play in Scott's mind as he carefully places the glasses on Herman's closed eyes. Scott slowly backs away from Herman as two Black Panther Party members close the casket. Herman, his life-long struggle for true equality and justice for the oppressed people of the world, laid to rest.

The sermon speaker returns and asks his audience to stand to make a silent prayer for Herman. Scott raises himself from his chair, lowers his head and closes his eyes as the voices around him say prayers for Herman, his family, the continuing struggle for social justice and true equality. Within the pitch black of Scott's closed eyes, a mirage of Herman walking out of a pair of large iron gates appears before him. Herman cracks a large smile across his face and tells Scott the final words of the beautiful poem he wrote in solitary confinement, *A Defined Voice*, "the louder my voice, the deeper they bury me! Free all political prisoners, prisoners of war, prisoners of consciousness." Scott opens his eyes and finds himself alone in the community center. Everyone has already left. Scott lets out a deep sigh and walks toward the exit. He pushes the glass doors open. A flash of bright, Louisiana sunlight shines upon Scott's face. Scott reflects on the brief vision he had, the final words Herman told him. As soon as Scott takes his first steps onto the concrete pathway, feelings of grief and remorse begin to envelop his heart. Scott realizes the meaning of his vision of Herman and his final words. Herman wanted Scott to honor his struggle, but to continue his fight and to assist those freedom fighters still imprisoned. A light smile grows on Scott's face as he looks up in the clear sky with his blue eyes. He holds his head high knowing that Herman's struggle has not passed with him. The struggle for true freedom and quality lives within Scott, and within everyone else.

Darker than with my eyes closed

Thousands of pebbles
Stacked atop the wave-forged stones
Below that the sand

Fits and starts of song
Waves crashing on rocky beach
A Bossa Nova

How did I get here?
A valid, futile question
Better not to ask

Kelly A. Harrison

Collective moment

Sooty shearwaters
Run along the water's edge,
Feet slapping, slapping.

The humpback rises,
a monolith before me.
We two, curious.

The breath: anchovies.
Its air is my air; mine, its.
The birds, our witness.

Ana Filomena Andrun

Early poise

Daring fresh lovely
Morning dive, into heart's desire
Earth pulses under me

Patient in love
Tall and bright, infinite in hope
I wait for wonders

Rich with cosmic chance
Silence like never before.
A day not yet lived.

Steve "Spike" Wong

Breaking good

B ruce Lee had been dead for six years already by the time I arrived, entirely unplanned, in a sleepy, tiny, undeveloped and, as I discovered, uninformed Italian coastal village nestled alongside the Ligurian Sea. It was what every footloose wanderer wanted in Italy: a small, ragtag collection of old streets and older buildings, a café or two and no restaurants, vineyards crawling up the hillside, and a curving, empty beach sitting calmly under a blazing sun. I checked into a ramshackle pensione and headed straight for some down time on the beach, picking up a loaf of bread, some mortadella and a bottle of wine along the way. A quick dip in the sea cleared off the day's travelling, and I settled in for a long, leisurely dinner.

"Bruce Lee! Bruce Lee!" Awakened from a wine-infused Italian reverie, I was accosted by a gang of tiny Italian kids whirling and jumping and twisting through the air. This approach was surely a joke, but the look in their dirt-smeared, sand-encrusted faces showed respect, admiration and worse, genuine recognition. They jumped up and down, mimicking side kicks and flying through the air, screaming and yelling like Italian cats caught in an alleyway dumpster. They pushed and shoved one another and continued their awkward side- and front-kicking with wild abandon in attempt to impress me. In my youth, Bruce Lee had been "the man" for us socially awkward and downtrodden Chinese-Americans who were looking for anything and anyone Chinese to improve our self-respect and social cachet. Indeed, Lee's intense kung fu image had pushed me into the martial arts during my high school years. Bruce Lee, the man, the legend, my Chinese brother. I had studied hard and trained harder, and I had thought I was getting somewhere in life but this was only the naiveté of teenhood. But now I was somewhere, in an Italian hamlet with a coterie of unwashed kids yelling "Bruce Lee, Bruce Lee!" These urchins wouldn't believe anything else. They wanted lessons, so I taught them how to punch and block, trap and sweep. Through it all they screamed bloody murder. And finally, after some miscommunication and miming, they pushed the smallest one of their number to the forefront and I did a flying side kick over him. Shouts and cheers from the assembled gang gave him hero status for being the one that Bruce Lee had flown over.

A few of them, called by the same mysterious force that compels certain birds to fly in formation, suddenly turned and ran off. They came back with a large stick. It was a small branch, really, a random piece of some tree that somehow ended up nearby on this very beach. It was the kind that always breaks in the movies when the hero hits it, but almost never in real life because the stringy layers won't allow that. Watching them pretend to chop it into pieces was the most animated humor I'd seen in some time, but through their hand pointing and eye movements, I soon realized that they wanted me to chop this branch in half. My first thought: Cool! My first sober thought: no fucking way. Though it was dry, wood like this had its own stubborn defense against being split by a human hand. I didn't want to disappoint them, yet I didn't want to turn the legend of Bruce Lee into the story of some Chinese-American who was thought to be him letting down an entire generation of local rug rats. But I especially didn't want to hurt myself. As I stood there scanning all these excited kids, I felt like a fraud for feeling like I couldn't do what they wanted. They were all there, hero-worshippers at the Temple of Hollywood, holding on to every part of the branch except for a three-foot section in the middle, waiting for me—no, Bruce Lee—to annihilate every molecule of that barren branch, and in one fell swoop. I took one very nervous breath and looked into the distance. The sun was setting, the heat beginning to dissipate a bit prior to stealing away on the breeze, the light that photographers call the "magic hour" illumined the eager young faces, and "What the hell," I thought, "I have another hand should I break my right one." In the pebbly sand, I positioned myself carefully. I gauged the length and angle of the strike. I breathed deeply again and again, centering myself for a supreme moment of focus. Every voice stilled. My hand moved, swiftly, surely, powerfully, quickly, precisely, and intently. Somewhere in the cosmos, Bruce Lee began laughing.

About the Authors

Adnan Adnan is originally from Jessore, Bangladesh. He is a creative nonfiction M.F.A. candidate at San José State University. In 2001, he published a book of poetry in Bengali. He is currently working on a memoir, *The Family Fables*. His works have appeared in the *Flash Fiction World*, *Mukto-Mona*, *The Rumpus*, *Reed magazine*, and *Two@SJSU*.

Ana Filomena Andrun is a student of life. People are her inspiration, and their beauty her muse. Her writings are her gifts to the world, a symbol of gratitude for days wondrous and wholesome. She is here to love all hearts that come her way, see them blossom into unstoppable, unbounded beings, in celebration of themselves.

Kristen Austin wrote her first autobiographical novel by age 13, only to discover it kinda sucked. However, her love for writing persists. She teaches English & Creative Writing at Los Gatos High, raises her two children Gabriel and Ava in Los Gatos, and spends time in San Francisco with her favorite wordsmith ever.

Linda Bakke is a Cuban-Korean and Ephemeral-Irish writer whose myriad heritage manifests into a rabidity for storytelling and blissful reclamation of identity. California provides vibrant context to her writing. After years in the visual arts; she is currently an undergraduate student of creative writing at San Francisco State.

Terry Barr's essays have appeared widely in such journals as *Full Grown People, Graze, Sport Literate, Compose, Four Ties Lit Review, Quail Bell Magazine*, and *Blue Lyra Review*. He teaches Creative Nonfiction at Presbyterian College and lives in Greenville, SC, with his family.

Carlos Barron is a first generation American of Mexican descent with an altruistic streak, delusions of grandeur, and a flair for the sarcastic. He dreams of making a positive impact on the world, or at least being proclaimed the single greatest writer in the history of the universe, while working on his third collegiate degree.

Melissa Becker is too wise to be young, too young to be wise. Color brings us to life; she just experiences the full spectrum all at once.

Jesi Bender is a writer and artist living in upstate New York. She is a librarian at a local university whose interests include inevitable tragedies, the grey scale, dissonance, and books.

Bri Bruce is an editor, graphic designer, and publisher from Santa Cruz, California. She holds a bachelor's degree in writing from UC Santa Cruz. Her work has appeared in *The Sun Magazine*, *The Soundings Review*, and *The Monterey Poetry Review*. Bruce is the award-winning author of *The Weight of Snow*.

Tess Crescini received her Master of Arts degree in Engaged Humanities and the Creative Life with emphasis in Depth Psychology at Pacifica Graduate Institute in an effort to unblock her creativity. She was born in the Philippines and enjoys writing about her hyphenated identity as a Filipina-American in San José, California.

Sage Curtis graduated from San José State University as a double major in Creative Writing and Journalism. Primarily a poet, Sage attended writing programs at UC Berkeley and CSU Monterey and is pursuing her MFA. While at SJSU, she worked as a reporter, features editor, and production editor at the Spartan Daily and studied abroad in Germany.

Steve Cushman received an MFA in Creative Writing from UNC-Greensboro. He's published two novels, *Portisville* and

Heart With Joy, as well as the short story collection, *Fracture City*. His debut poetry chapbook, *Hospital Work*, was published last year. Cushman currently works in IT at Moses Cone Memorial Hospital in Greensboro.

Maria D'Avolio is a mother, writer, and hula hoop champ.

Christopher Danaher has previously received honorable mention in a haiku contest sponsored by the Mainichi Shimbun in Japan. He currently lives in Pittsburgh, Pennsylvania, with his wife, the sculptor Jessica Danaher, and their beautiful daughter.

Kate Evans' memoir, *Arriving Again and Again (an odyssey of love, sex, spirit and travel)* is forthcoming. Her fiction, poetry and essays are widely published. A former university writing teacher, she is a private writing coach. She lives in California Baja Sur, Mexico.

Ashley Florimonte is a poet and short story writer of both fiction and non-fiction. She graduated with a degree in English from San José State University and spends her free time writing, stretching, and laughing uncontrollably.

Susan Forrest is a Santa Cruz actress, published playwright and two-time winner of Actors' Theatre Ten Minute Play Festival. She has also written and directed ten plays for Northern Castle Theatre for Children.

Brian Foss is sort of retired in Santa Cruz with his wife Marcia Areias. He has been writing poetry for family and friends for 30 years and hopes that all two hundred of the bad poems that Billy Collins says every poet must get through are all behind him. He characterizes his writing as the seriously whimsical school of poetry, or the whimsically serious school.....or such.....or whatever.

Nan Friedley is a retired special education teacher living in Riverside, California. She taught in Indiana and southern California. A collection of her poetry was included in the 2013 *Inlandia Anthology* and the *Orangelandia* publication.

Erica Goss is the Poet Laureate of Los Gatos, CA. She won the 2011 Many Mountains Moving Poetry Contest, and was nominated for the Pushcart Prize (2010, 2013). Her chapbook, *Wild Place*, was published in 2012 by Finishing Line Press. Erica is a columnist for Connotation Press.

Sebastien Grace is a poet, author, and reluctant high school student. They live in Santa Cruz, California.

Kelly A. Harrison is a writer living in San José, CA. She's currently working on The Body Remembered, a novel about body memory, sexual abuse, and their effects on the birth experience. After spending years in the high-tech industry, Kelly changed careers and is now teaching at San José State University.

Mark Heinlein's book, *Everything We Call Ordinary*, was published in 2014 by Tourane Poetry Press. "*Family, Culture and How a Poet Makes His Bread*," his TEDx Talk, was performed in 2013. Born in Indiana, he is a fishmonger and lives in San José, California.

Belinda Hopkinson is a professional editor and writer; she is also in the process of becoming a movement teacher and movement therapist. She is a lifelong lover of the outdoors, words, music, the human voice, and dance.

Tram Huynh is a 2013 graduate of San José State University. After graduation, she went on a pilgrimage to India, amongst other Buddhist landmarks, which was her inspiration for her piece in *Three*. Tram hopes to travel more to build up her "spice bag" to flavor her future writing.

Victoria M. Johnson writes, blogs, and makes short films and micro documentaries. She is the author of five books.

Morgan Marie Kelly, 18, from Hong Kong living in Los Gatos, California.

Kylie Kenner appreciated literature of brevity from an early age, gravitating towards short works of fiction (such as *The Very Hungry Caterpillar*) at her earliest signs of literacy. When she isn't imparting her wisdom on future generations as a teacher and author, Kylie enjoys cat videos, crafts and travel.

Tom Leikam can mostly likely be found on the trails of the Central Coast with his camera in hand taking pictures of the awe inspiring nature. Each journey fulfills the quest of a life filled with wonder.

Zac Locke lives in West Hollywood, California. Thanks to his wife, one-year-old son, and Boston Terrier, he currently suffers from chronic cuteness overload. He published a novella, *Beverlywood: Sex, Murder, Existentialism (A Tuesday in Los Angeles)*.

Gayle Lubeck holds a B.A. in Advertising from San José State University, as well as having completed coursework in their English and Comparative Literature Master's program. She has published two academic papers that are included in CSULA's Significations Conference proceedings. She is a non-fiction writer residing in Salinas, California.

Kathleen Maliksi is a dreamer and a lover of words, with a particular affinity for Russian literature. She grew up in Washington and in the Philippines and now calls the Bay Area home. She's an English major at San José State University and is currently embarking on the journey of writing a novel.

Jesse Mardian is an MFA student at San José State University. His short stories and flash fictions have been published in *Riprap*, *Four Ties Review*, *Fiction Southwest*, and *Two@SJSU* among others. Currently, he is writing his thesis, a picaresque novel set in Sevilla, Spain.

Alex Marroquin is a Californian with a heart and soul for the people across the globe and at home. He is currently studying Creative Writing and works as a peer tutor at San José State University. His biggest dream is to become an influential novelist, poet, and screenwriter.

Mary Martine is deeply committed to mental health education and advocacy. She lives in the Bay Area with her two children.

Jane Matchak is addicted to drinking coffee and falls in love with every dog she has ever met.

Heather Matley is a writer from Los Gatos, California, who can't help but immerse herself in anything and everything art-related. While trying to survive her freshman year at Chapman University and figure out exactly what this whole school thing is all about, she works on developing her own creative style.

Gregory Mayo is a professional problem solver.

Jan McCutcheon is currently working on a memoir that is a dark comedy about family, death, and the Mafia—that is, when she is not doing or talking about CrossFit. She lives in San José with her engineer husband, snarky teenage daughter, and very good dog.

Jeri McCutcheon is the third daughter, the twisted sister. She is freakishly flexible, extensively tattooed, and inspired to express creativity through writing, photography, yoga, and martial arts. She also has an odd desire to develop a circus act where she contorts into a tiny box.

Rose Marie McNair will forever seek to know more about the art of living.

Tonya McQuade wrote her first poems in elementary school—though then it was rhyme, not haiku! At the University of California, Santa Barbara, she turned her attention to non-fiction writing as a journalist for the *Daily Nexus*. Now, she teaches

English at Los Gatos High School and tries to get others to write in various forms.

Shauna Miller, aka Dread, is a photographer extrodinaire who is putting in her hours in the corporate work world until she can make a living shooting people.

Roger Mock is a retired educator with experience from kindergarten to university. He enjoys photography, walking, drawing, singing, and reading biographies. At age 72, he has committed to learning to play the piano.

Ume Naqvi is a student and SuperMom (of three children) by day, when she isn't busy saving the world she writes poetry, fiction, and creative nonfiction. She currently writes feature and lifestyle articles for *Azizah* and serves as contributing editor.

Sarju Naran is a partner in a San José law firm. He enjoys spending time with his six and three year old daughters, and is two credits shy of earning his Masters in Karaoke and Hip Hop.

Nahida S. Nisa sometimes wishes she were a more practical woman, but she is not practical enough to wish it often.

Shirindokht Nourmanesh is a scholar of poetry and prose, proficient in both Persian and English. She is a writer, an artist, a translator, and an independent researcher. Shirindokht teaches composition courses and conducts writing workshops at San José State University.

Alexander Papoulias is a native Californian and first-generation American. "The Gold Country" was written for his father Dimitri, who was a tough son of a bitch.

Pranita Patel is an educator, artist, and writer. The purpose of her work is to heal, transform and strengthen individuals and communities. Her work is spiritually based and is inspired by eastern thought and the Divine Feminine.

Brandy Pech is a student of the world.

Tara Phillips worked as a Radiologic Technologist for fourteen years, and currently works part time at a children's hospital in Palo Alto, California. She graduated with a BA in English and Creative Writing at SJSU in May, 2013. In 2012, she earned a Catherine Urban Scholarship for writing and in 2013, the Lois King Thore Short Story Scholarship. Her work has been published in *Two@SJSU*.

Meg Pokrass is the author of "Damn Sure Right" (Press 53, 2011) a collection of flash fiction. Her stories have appeared in numerous online and print publications, including T*he Literar-*

ian, storySouth, Failbetter, Gigantic, PANK, Mississippi Review, and *McSweeney's*. She currently serves as an associate editor for Frederick Barthelme's *New World Writing*.

Yasmin Ramirez is a native El Pasoan. Her work has appeared in various publications such as *HUIZACHE* and *Cream City Review*. Currently, she is completing her first book.

Kate Reid is a predominately non-fiction writer whose work for *Three* aims to offer another perspective—one in which a teenager can spend days at the helm of a sailboat preoccupied only by deciding whether bobbing circles in the distance are fishing floats, or sea turtles.

Sarah Lyn Rogers is an MFA candidate at San José State University, where her emphases are fiction and poetry. When she's not writing, Sarah is Assistant Fiction Editor for *The Rumpus*. She also works as a writing mentor, copyeditor, and layout manager for *Society of Young Inklings*, a nonprofit writing community and publishing imprint for young writers.

Jessica Sauceda loves writing, hiking, coffee and deep conversations. One of her favorite quotes is Maya Angelou's, "There is no greater agony than bearing an untold story inside of you." She aspires to empower others to express and heal themselves through writing. She hopes to one day walk the Camino de Santiago.

Evelyn A. So's poetry has appeared in literary journals such as *Measure: A Review of Formal Poetry, Red Wheelbarrow (National Edition), Gingerbread House,* and *Adanna Literary Journal,* among others. Her nonfiction is included in the anthology *Al-Mutanabbi Street Starts Here* edited by Beau Beausoleil and Deema Shehabi.

Janie M. Vasquez was born and raised in Watsonville, CA. She married her Junior High school sweetheart, and together they raised six children. She has taken her obstacles and personal life experiences and transformed those moments into words.

Daniel Wallock is an award-winning author who was born with seven life-threatening heart conditions. He dreams of sharing his stories. A college student in Vermont, he is currently experimenting with shorter forms of nonfiction and poetry. His heart and love for life are at the core of his work.

Steve "Spike" Wong indulges in mountain sports and constant acts of imagination.

Bryan Wong (no relation to Spike) is a twenty-one year veteran of the fire service and part-time beach lifeguard during the summer months. He marvels at the acceleration of time since the birth of his daughter seven years ago.

Bob Woodward's life cycle to date includes a stint in the corporate world followed by four decades career as a freelance writer/photographer with a few editorial positions along the way. He lives in Bend, Oregon where he served as the town's mayor from 1997 to 1999.

Candice Wynne spent decades through the gauntlet of her life when one day she decided it was time to step across the threshold of conventionality to discover the world one country, one train ride, one curious footstep at a time. She holds an MFA in Narrative Nonfiction at San José State University.

Tim Yee is a bucket-list performer extraordinaire.

Acknowledgments

Spike gratefully acknowledges that a boatload of free and powerful spirits have contributed to his well-being and creativity. Chief among these are his parents, Ernie and Alice, who have always let him run free; his wife Debbie for enlightened support, and his children Devin and Margo, for adding zest and inspiration to his life. And to the rest of the boatload, Spike remembers you all and is deeply thankful for your acceptance, understanding, and shared tomfoolery.

Jan would like to thank her family, who have been an endless source of love, laughter, and support, as well as often providing the source material for her best stories.

Afterword

One.

Please participate.
Submission guidelines at www.pushpenpress.com.

www.ingramcontent.com/pod-product-compliance
Lightning Source LLC
Chambersburg PA
CBHW031222260626
47169CB00007B/2155